THE Presidential Quotient

Wayne
Samuel
Kurzeja

Chicago Review Press
• Chicago •

Cover and puzzler design by Anistatia Renard

Library of Congress Cataloging in Publication Data

Kurzeja, Wayne Samuel, 1946–
    The presidential quotient.

    Bibliography: p.
    1. Presidents—United States—Miscellanea.
2. Presidents—United States—Anecdotes, facetiae, satire, etc.
I. Title.
E176.1.K87 1984   973'.09'92   84-7737
ISBN 0-914091-53-0

To my father who taught me how to laugh and to dream.

And to Lou, my high school sweetheart.

Contents

Author's Preface

Presidents are fascinating people. The thirty-nine men who have held this highest position in the land each brought a unique personality to the job, and left his own special mark on history. It is this personal element of presidential history that has fascinated me, more than the history of dates and treaties. Henry Adams once said, "I am a professor of history...but I rejoice that I never remember a date."

Yet even more striking than the uniqueness of the presidents' personalities are the similarities between them. Can it be a coincidence that so many presidents had sickly childhoods? That so many were middle children? That so many loved sweet potatoes? Or can such shared characteristics be used to define a general profile of the Presidential Personality?

The Presidential Quotient Quiz outlines the common characteristics that constitute the Presidential Personality. Anyone can take the quiz to discover how much presidential character is lurking in each of us. Sex and race are no barrier to the Presidential Quotient; I believe that in the next few decades there will be female and minority presidents.

Clarence Darrow once remarked, "History repeats itself. That's one of the things wrong with history." In the chapters that follow the quiz, I have attempted to pick out those recurring factors that influenced the men who became president. Some chapters, such as "Brothers and Sisters" and "Children," also deal with the effect of the presidents' personalities on those close to them.

The Presidential Puzzlers sprinkled throughout the book are startling reminders that history does indeed repeat itself, and that some presidential patterns are amazingly similar.

Is your personality the stuff of which presidents are made?

Acknowledgements

Many people have been exceedingly generous in giving me their time and effort in order that I might write this volume. The Honorable Robert McClory and the late John Roosevelt put me into contact with many of their friends and acquaintances. Jonathan Roosevelt gathered together the Theodore Roosevelt clan for a group interview. I am also grateful to presidential relatives John Quincy Adams V, John Coolidge, Lyon Miles, Senator Robert Taft, Jr., Frances Payne Tyler and Lawrence Washington.

In gathering the wealth of information necessary for such a book, I must thank Drs. Thomas Glimp and Jeffrey Lieblich for medical sources, historian Donald C. McGlothlin for checking for accuracy, and Jayne Pitney and Eric Quackenbush for being on the lookout for any information I might be able to use. My brother Gary was extremely helpful in listening to ideas and readings of chapters as I worked on them. Both Ken Dachman and Curt Matthews encouraged me as soon as I brought the idea for the book to them. My editor, Julie Rubin, was sensitive and understanding throughout the writing and rewriting. And most of all I wish to thank my wife, Lou, for her help and patience and for logging easily as many hours as I did toward the completion of this book.

Shortly after this man was elected president, the nation was hit with the devastating depression of the thirties. Although many experts believed that the depression was created from factors that existed before he became president, most Americans began linking the president's name to the depression. After only one term in office, he failed to win reelection and left office in disgrace. He died of natural causes in '62, twenty-one years after leaving the White House. Who was this unfortunate president?

1

The Presidential Quotient Quiz

What is your PQ? Answer the forty questions on the following pages, add up your score, and compare it to the chart at the end of the answers to the quiz. Not only will you be able to find out if you have what it takes to be president of the United States, but you will also be able to tell what kind of president you might become: a Lincoln? a Roosevelt? a Harding?

Remember, there is no right answer or wrong answer, just the most likely answer for the majority of presidents.

1. When I was born my father was:

    A. 24 years old or younger
    B. Between the ages of 25 and 35
    C. Between the ages of 36 and 45
    D. 45 years old or older

2. When I was born my mother was:

A. 24 years old or younger
B. Between the ages of 25 and 35
C. Between the ages of 36 and 45
D. 45 years old or older

3. My birthdate falls during:

    A. January or April
    B. May, June, or September
    C. July, August, or December
    D. October or November

4. My name is:

    A. From my mother's side of the family
    B. From my father's side of the family
    C. Partly from my mother's and partly from my father's family
    D. My last name is the only name I share with other members of the family

5. My brothers and sisters are:

    A. Younger than I am
    B. Older than I am
    C. Younger and older than I am
    D. I have no brothers and sisters

6. My birthsite was:

    A. A large city
    B. A medium city

    C. A small town
    D. A rural area

7. My father was:

    A. A professional person
    B. A tradesperson
    C. A laborer
    D. Self-employed

8. I like my name:

    A. Because it's a family name
    B. Because it is different
    C. Because it doesn't call attention to me
    D. I don't like my name at all

9. I feel my childhood and teenage years were about as happy as anyone else's were:

    A. Rarely or never true
    B. Sometimes true
    C. Often true
    D. Usually or always true

10. I could best typify my mother as:

    A. A loving housewife and supportive helpmate to my father
    B. An intelligent and strong-willed independent thinker
    C. An ardent gossiper and a good cook

D. I barely knew my mother

11. My mother and I have:

    A. Always disagreed with each other
    B. Always been much closer than my friends are to their mothers
    C. Occasionally disagreed, but usually are pretty good friends
    D. Rarely spent much time together

12. My father was the kind of man who:

    A. Was intelligent and kind, but never reached his full potential
    B. Was a frustrated and somewhat self-destructive person
    C. Was so talented he made me feel inferior
    D. I barely knew my father

13. During my school years, I repeatedly missed days of school due to illness.

    A. Rarely or never true
    B. Sometimes true
    C. Often true
    D. Usually or always true

14. People who know me say I had every advantage as I grew up.

    A. Rarely or never true

B. Sometimes true
C. Often true
D. Usually or always true

15. If I wanted to go to college, my family:

    A. Would encourage me, but couldn't afford to pay for it
    B. Would encourage me and would pay for it
    C. Would discourage me, but could have afforded it
    D. Would discourage me, but couldn't have afforded it anyhow

16. When I meet people of the opposite sex to whom I am attracted, I:

    A. Turn on the charm
    B. Become uncomfortable around them
    C. Try to get to know them somehow
    D. Avoid them

17. I can remember the names of every person I ever fell in love with.

    A. Rarely or never true
    B. Sometimes true
    C. Often true
    D. Usually or always true

18. In looking for a spouse, I expect:

    A. Someone to take care of me
    B. A business partner

C. A companion
D. An intellectual equal

19. When looking for someplace to live, I want:

    A. A home that truly expresses my personality
    B. The most impressive house I can afford
    C. Just a comfortable place to eat and sleep
    D. Someplace that I can resell for a good profit

20. When it comes to animals I:

    A. Don't like them around my house
    B. Can take them or leave them
    C. Would like my home to have at least one pet
    D. Am usually surrounded by them at home

21. In the last three weeks I ate the most of:

    A. A variety of expertly prepared foods
    B. My favorite foods
    C. Whatever was available
    D. I have no idea

22. If asked to speak in front of a large group, I would:

    A. Refuse right from the start
    B. Probably get sick the night before the speech
    C. Do my best to prepare an interesting speech
    D. Probably end up talking longer than the group
       expected

23. At a medium-sized birthday party for an acquaintance, I would:

    A. Try to talk to everyone at some time during the evening
    B. Do my best to meet the most attractive member of the opposite sex
    C. Find my closest friends and spend the night talking to them
    D. Spend most of my time helping in the kitchen or choosing records

24. When I know I'll have to eat lunch alone in a restaurant:

    A. I kid with the waiter and watch the other diners
    B. I bring along something to read or study
    C. I am self-conscious, so I just eat and leave
    D. I never eat alone in restaurants

25. At a formal dinner party, I would:

    A. Constantly worry if I were using the utensils properly
    B. Enjoy it most if I sat in between two really close friends
    C. Enjoy the food and the conversation whether or not I could take part in most of it
    D. Probably talk more than I would eat

26. On a long ocean cruise, I would bring:

    A. Casual clothes, writing paper and a dictionary

   B. Sportswear, novels and suntan lotion
   C. Comfortable clothes, histories and biographies, and motion sickness pills
   D. Evening clothes, romances and cologne

27. I work best on a project when:

   A. A group of us share the workload equally
   B. Someone supervises and encourages me
   C. I can delegate small portions of the job to others
   D. I can be by myself with all the resources handy

28. If three co-workers and I were being considered for a new position within the company, I would:

   A. Try to have myself removed from consideration
   B. Suggest one of the other people as more qualified
   C. Accept the position reluctantly if I won it
   D. Aggressively pursue the new job

29. On days when I don't have to work or run errands:

   A. I work on my hobbies or crafts
   B. I stay around the house and watch TV
   C. I curl up with a good book and read until I'm finished
   D. I do something outside

30. My successful business has had two fires in the last five years, and the insurance company now refuses to insure it. I would:

    A. Rebuild in the same location
    B. Rebuild in a different location
    C. Sell the business to someone else and start working for him or her
    D. Forget the business and look for a new job

31. I'm on vacation, and I meet a business owner who wants to place a large order for products manufactured by the company I work for. I am not a salesman, so I:

    A. Avoid the business owner for the rest of the vacation
    B. Give the owner the office number of the company I work for
    C. Take the order and discuss it with the office when I get back in town
    D. Take the order and call it in to the office

32. If I have done my very best at a certain task, but I fail, I feel:

    A. It can't be done
    B. I can always rely on help from my friends to get it done
    C. It wasn't that important to me anyhow
    D. Eventually I will succeed

33. You will find me working late hours or weekends at my job:

    A. Rarely or never true
    B. Sometimes true

C. Often true
D. Usually or always true

34. When I think about retirement I:

    A. Will be busy doing things I never had time for
    B. Know it's for other people but not for me
    C. Will finally be able to do what I want: sleep late every day
    D. Look forward to taking it easy

35. I can best describe my life as:

    A. A delicious bowl of cherries
    B. A bowl of cherries, some sweet and some sour
    C. A bowl of cherries, all of them sour
    D. A bowl of cherry pits

36. Throughout my schooling, my grades were:

    A. Just passing
    B. Average
    C. Above average
    D. At the top of the class

37. In high school, I was elected:

    A. Valedictorian or president of the class
    B. Most likely to succeed
    C. Most friendly
    D. I hated every minute of high school and left as quickly as possible

38. My first job was:

   A. Delivering papers or something similar as a child or teenager
   B. Working for my father while still young
   C. The first job I could get right out of high school
   D. In my chosen field after completing my degree

39. I think "Love at first sight" is:

   A. An immature and childish concept
   B. Impossible; you must know people well to love them
   C. Possible for some people, but not for me
   D. The best description of how I fell in love

40. I usually:

   A. Go to bed early and get up early
   B. Go to bed early and get up late
   C. Go to bed late and get up early
   D. Go to bed late and get up late

This president became a partner in his father's farm well before he expressed any desire to enter politics. His father's nickname was "Peanuts." His younger brother also helped on the farm. When his Southern Baptist grandmother saw his blue uniform after he had joined the service, she refused to let him into the house, well remembering the War Between the States and those blue-coated Yankees. This man was a Democrat and was president in this century. Who was he?

2

Mothers

Every mother wants her son to become president, but no mother wants her son to become a politician.

—*William McKinley*

One day Jimmy Carter went into his mother's bedroom, sat on the chair, rested his feet up on the bed, and announced, "Mom, I've decided that I'm going to run for president." "President of what?" she inquired calmly. "President of the United States," he answered. "Jimmy," she said, "Get your shoes off the bed."

Any one of the ten women who lived to see their sons actually become president of the United States might have had the same reaction when her son announced his intention. Even with all the faith these women had in their sons' abilities, it was probably hard for them to believe that the tiny babies they had held in their arms would reach the highest office in the land. Martha Truman, Harry's mother, once said, "I never thought that Harry would become president." She quickly added, "He'll make a good one, though."

The thirty-nine women who produced presidents of the United States were, by and large, strong-willed, educated women who spent a lot of time with their young children. Their interest in the welfare of their children was so strong, in fact, that many of them produced what might be called "Momma's boys."

When Democratic kingmakers asked young Franklin Roosevelt to run in his first election for the state legislature, he said he would have to ask his mother first. The political bosses were not impressed and this comment almost ended his political career before it started. Franklin Roosevelt's mother, Sara, was not one to let her son leave the nest too soon. When he was supposed to leave for Groton at the age of twelve, Sara kept him home with her for an additional two years. She could not bear to let him go, so she sent him to schools closer to home. Thus he attended Groton for four years instead of the usual six. When it was time for Franklin to attend Harvard, Sara found a place close by and moved near the campus so that she could keep an eye on him. In later years, when Franklin and Eleanor were married, she set up house for them, picking out furniture, hiring servants, and doing all the other things that young housewives enjoy doing for themselves. This did not much endear her to the new bride. Years later when the "young couple" moved into the White House, Sara was on hand to help pick out the curtains.

Rosalyn Carter, wife of Jimmy Carter, also had to learn to cope with her mother-in-law. When Jimmy was elected governor of Georgia, Miss Lillian moved into the governor's mansion with them. Rosalyn soon concluded that one lady in the house was enough, and insisted that her mother-in-law leave.

Although Sara Roosevelt and Lillian Carter never fully approved of their daughters-in-law, they never allowed their reservations to become public. And both mothers proved to be effective campaigners during their sons' bids for the presidency.

The ultimate campaigner, however, was Rose Kennedy. Already seasoned at political life before she married John Kennedy's father, Joseph, Rose was undoubtedly an asset to her son's campaign. She was the daughter of Boston politico John "Honey Fitz" Fitzgerald. Rose was well accustomed to meeting popes, presidents, and kings, as well as the "deros," a term for her father's supporters from the "dear old North end" of Boston. In later years, she told reporters that her children were sung political lullabies when they were babies. She expected impressive political achievements from her sons.

Hannah Nixon was so proud of her son Richard that she kept a back-lit transparent photograph of him hung on her living room wall. Ida Eisenhower took a calmer pride in her son Dwight's achievements. When asked by a reporter if she were proud of her son, she replied, "Which one? I'm proud of them all."

Although Rebekah Johnson, mother of Lyndon Baines Johnson, did not live to see her son become president, she did see him win the congressional seat that her father had lost many years before. She wrote, "I love you, I believe in you and I expect great things of you, Lyndon. How happy it would have made my noble father to know that the first born of his first born would achieve the position he desired." Although Lyndon Johnson's own father won a congressional seat, he failed to win reelection and was a great disappointment to Lyndon's mother. She obviously expected here son to do better. Nowhere in her letter to Lyndon did she even mention his father.

Many presidential mothers, in fact, seem to have applied strong pressure on their sons to do what their own husbands and fathers had failed to do. William Howard Taft's mother is known to have urged her son to do what her husband had only aspired to: become chief justice of the Supreme Court. Even the presidency may have been a disappointment to this mother. And it was William Taft's wife, rather than Taft himself, who wanted him to become president. He sided with his mother: "I don't hesitate to say that I would rather have been chief justice than president." After his presidential term he did become chief justice, which must have given him great satisfaction, even though his mother did not live to see her great ambition for him fulfilled.

Of course, other presidential mothers set much more modest goals for their sons. Elizabeth Harrison, mother of President Benjamin Harrison, simply said to her budding politician, "I hope you will be prudent in your Diet...and abstain from cucumbers." It is not recorded whether President Harrison abstained from eating cucumbers, but most likely he did, as many presidents made a point of listening to their mothers' advice. James K. Polk, eleventh president of the United States, once said, "Mother, I have never in my life disobeyed you." Maybe he should have listened instead to Benjamin Harrison's mother, since James K. Polk died of a stomach ailment.

Harry Truman's mother, Martha, had this advice for her son, advice that he undoubtedly took: "Just belong to the key of B-natural." Elizabeth Jackson once told her son, Andrew Jackson, "You can make friends by being honest, and you can keep them by being steadfast...None will respect you more than you respect yourself."

A very high level of self-respect and self-confidence is a prerequisite for any aspirant to the presidency; our often savage political process simply weeds out men with overly tender egos. Presidential-sized egos were nurtured from an early age by mothers who set high moral, if not high political, standards for their children. If some of those mothers had a hard time letting go of their ambitious sons, it was a small price to pay for the attention they lavished on them in the crucial years of their development.

First First Family Problems

General George Washington, in the midst of the war

with Great Britain, had more than his share of problems. Congress had no more money to give him, and almost all of his personal funds had gone into the war effort. He was very close to being destitute. He had to cope with dwindling supplies, failing troop morale, battle fatigue, and political pressures from people who had no idea how to fight a war. And worst of all, he had to deal with his mother, Mary Ball Washington.

She had not wanted him to go into the army in the first place. "There was no end of my troble while George was in the army," she wrote later. And although she was quite well off, she protested that none of her sons ever helped her financially. "I never lived soe pore in my Life," she complained in a letter to her son Jack. George's response was indignant. "She has had a great deal of money from me at times, as can be made appear by my books," he told his brother, "and [I] have paid many hundred pounds to her in cash."

Despite George's protestations, Mary continued to complain to friends and strangers alike that he treated her pitifully. Finally, in 1781, a group of George's enemies in the Virginia Assembly seized on her grievances as means to politically embarrass and humiliate him. The Virginia Assembly made it known publicly that it was planning to grant a pension to the mother of General Washington because she was "in great want."

When George Washington learned of this plan, he was furious. In a statement to a friend, Washington said, "Before I left Virginia, I answered all her calls for money, and since the period have directed my steward to do the same." He was very upset that his mother would be "receiving charity from the public." Fortunately, the Virginia Assembly withdrew its plan and the whole matter blew over. Would Washington have been elected president if everyone had thought that he neglected his poor mother?

Harry's Toughest Fight

Political opponents of Harry S Truman used tactics similar to those Washington's opponents had used; they tried to get at him through his mother. A savvy politician, Harry went out of his way to keep them from having the opportunity to do so. When he was Jackson County judge, a road was built that cut through his mother's farm. Harry decided that it would not be right to press the government to reimburse his mother for the property. Although other people in the community received payment for their land, Harry's mother did not. She later told a reporter, "I would have gotten eleven thousand dollars if my boy wasn't county judge."

And, in fact, as Harry rose in the political world, the financial reverses suffered by Martha only increased. Her difficulties reached a peak in 1940 when Harry was running for reelection to the United States Senate, his toughest fight. In that race, he was being accused of every kind of dishonesty by his opponents. Tom Pendergast, the political boss who helped put Harry in the Senate, was in jail for income tax evasion. Harry had no money and very little support for his reelection campaign. Every major newspaper in the state had endorsed his opponents. Senator Truman had to sleep in the car when he went from town to town to give campaign speeches because he had no money for hotels. He did not even have money for stamps to send letters to friends to ask them for money.

But worst of all, while Harry was fighting for his political life on the road, Martha was losing her house. Her mortgage payments had fallen behind, and Harry's enemies, getting wind of this opportunity to sabotage his career, forced foreclosure. Martha kept her difficulties to herself. What with all the problems Harry was having, she did not want to burden him with any more. Besides, she reasoned, even if her son were told about the foreclosure, he

18

would not be able to do anything about it, since he had no money. The mother of the United States senator from Missouri, who in less than five years would be the mother of the president of the United States, experienced the humiliation of being turned out onto the street with all her furniture and belongings.

When Harry Truman found out, he was furious, not only because his enemies had tried to get at him through his mother, but also because, had he known in time, he could have stopped the foreclosure. The farm was mortgaged for only thirty-five thousand dollars and was worth far more than that. He could easily have negotiated a second mortgage to pay off the amount in arrears. But it was too late; the damage was done. The only thing he was able to do was help his mother move. He still had an election to win.

Harry won that election by the slimmest of margins, in spite of all the pressure and problems. "It was the toughest election of my life," he later recalled. Eight years later, in 1948, when he was running for president against Thomas Dewey, the public found it amazing that he was able to persevere in the face of what most experts were sure was going to be a crushing defeat. But he knew that his toughest fight was already behind him.

Abe Lincoln's Roots

In the early 1850s when Abe Lincoln was "riding the circuit," traveling from court to court to argue cases for his clients, he told his law partner, William H. Herndon, a story that would keep historians arguing for years to come.

Herndon had noticed Lincoln's gloomy mood while they were riding out to handle a case in Petersburg, Illinois that involved an illegitimate child. Lincoln seemed to have unusually strong feelings about the case. Finally, he confided to his law partner that his mother was herself an illegitimate child, that she was the result of the attentions paid by a wealthy farmer to Lincoln's impoverished grandmother. Herndon kept Lincoln's comments secret until after Lincoln's death, at which point he decided to do some detective work. He sent out many letters to persons he believed had some family knowledge handed down over the years that might shed some light on the issue of Abe Lincoln's roots. In addition, he studied all available court records. He discovered that Nancy Hanks Lincoln was not the daughter of Joseph and Nancy Hanks, but their granddaughter. The Hanks' eldest daughter, Lucy, had had the child out of wedlock and had given her to her parents to raise. This information confirmed what Abe Lincoln had told Herndon many years before.

But something else even more startling came up during Herndon's investigation, something concerning the parentage of Abe Lincoln himself. Herndon never published this other discovery, as it was based on a rumor and could not be proven. He gave Lincoln's mother the benefit of the doubt. Still, he found it surprising that the rumor was so widespread among people who seemed to have inside knowledge.

Nancy Lincoln, as the story goes, was "sweet" on another man while she was married to Abe's father, Tom. Sometime in the spring of 1808, Nancy had relations with the man, and in February, 1809, she gave birth to a baby boy and named him Abraham after the boy's grandfather. It was rumored at the time that Tom Lincoln was not able to father children because, in William Herndon's own words, he had been "castrated, fixed, cut." This rumor, however, has never been proven.

The story further tells of a confrontation between the man and Tom Lincoln in which, during a scuffle, Tom bit off the tip of the man's nose. Years after that incident, it was said that a certain man often bragged around town that he had fathered Abraham Lincoln. His name was Abraham

Enloe. Even though most people in the small Kentucky town thought of him as a crackpot, he had one disturbing feature: he was missing the tip of his nose.

William Herndon once quoted Lincoln as saying, "Did you ever notice that bastards are generally smarter, shrewder, and more intellectual than others? Is it because [those qualities are] stolen?"

The Span of a Life

Josephine Mary Hannon was born in Acton, Massachusetts on October 31, 1865, the same year that Abraham Lincoln was assassinated. Her birthdate was exactly 260 days after the president's tragic death.

Josephine Mary Hannon Fitzgerald, as she later became, lived to see nineteen different United States presidents, one of whom was her grandson John F. Kennedy. She has the distinction of being the only woman in American history to have the opportunity to vote for her own grandson for president.

Mrs. Fitzgerald died on August 8, 1964, exactly 260 days after the assassination of John F. Kennedy.

Miss Lillian Meets the Challenge

Aides to President Jimmy Carter were concerned when they discovered that the president's mother had consented to an interview without their knowledge. The Carter staff had hoped to monitor any questions directed at the famous First Mother because no one on the staff believed that Miss Lillian would be able to field difficult questions from aggressive reporters. Staffers became even more apprehensive when they realized that the reporter scheduled to meet

21

Miss Lillian was one who was particularly critical of the Carter administration. Unable to stop the scheduled interview, Carter's people merely braced themselves for the possibility of an embarassing incident.

The interview seemed to go smoothly until the reporter questioned Miss Lillian about her son's statement that he would never lie to the American people. "Can you, as his mother, honestly say that he's never lied?" the reporter queried. "Oh, perhaps he has told a little white lie now and then," Miss Lillian answered. Carter's aides were visibly shaken when the reporter pushed further and asked exactly what the difference was between a little white lie and any other one. "Define a white lie for me," she demanded. Miss Lillian kept her composure and replied, "I'm not sure I can give you a definition, but I can give you an example. Do you remember when you came in the door a minute ago, and I told you how good you looked and how glad I was to see you?"

This president's father received a job from the Roosevelt administration because he had supported Franklin D. Roosevelt in his campaign for the presidency. The father was an Irish Catholic and a staunch Democrat. The son chose a Texan as a running mate for his eventually successful bid for the presidency. He was the first man to serve as president at his age. Who was this president?

3

Fathers

My father wasn't a failure; he produced a president of the United States.

—Harry S Truman

O ne might expect the fathers of the presidents to have been successful and politically sophisticated men, and this quite often has been the case. William Howard Taft's father, Alphonso, was ambassador to Austria-Hungary, attorney-general and secretary of war under Ulysses S. Grant. Jimmy Carter's father, Earl, served in the state legislature, as did both Lyndon Johnson's father and Calvin Coolidge's father. Franklin Pierce's father, Benjamin Pierce, was the governor of New Hampshire, and both John Tyler's father and William Henry Harrison's father were governors of Virginia. Harrison's father, Benjamin, also signed the Declaration of Independence. William Henry Harrison's son John Scott Harrison served in Congress and was the father of President Benjamin Harrison. Joseph P. Kennedy was a politically influential "first father" who had served as ambassador to Great Britain. Another former ambassador to Great Britain, President John Adams, lived to see his son John Quincy Adams also inaugurated president. This was the only time in American history that the son of a president also held that office.

But a surprising number of presidential fathers have been anything but successful and politically sophisticated. Two years before the birth of Millard Fillmore, his father, Nathaniel, purchased sight unseen from a traveling salesman a portion of land in Cayuga County, New York. He moved there with his wife, cleared the land and built a log cabin. Once they were settled, he attempted to farm the property but soon discovered that the land was mostly clay and was worthless for farming. It was on that soil that a future president, Millard Fillmore, was born.

Nathaniel Fillmore was not the only president's father to blame bad soil for his failure in farming. A little over a hundred years later, Richard Nixon's father, Frank, purchased ten acres of land thirty miles east of Los Angeles, California. He built a house, moved his family there and planted lemon tree seedlings which, due to poor soil conditions, never amounted to anything.

When Anne Neal married newly ordained Princeton graduate Reverend Richard Cleveland, his prospects were good. His successes, however, failed to materialize, and they spent their lives struggling from one small congregation to another. The Clevelands could not even afford to send their children to college, and young Grover Cleveland had to fend for himself.

Many first fathers who were in government held low level jobs or failed to advance. Lyndon Johnson's father, shortly before he married, was elected to the Texas state legislature. His wife had faith that he would go far, but only two short years after their marriage he was voted out of office and never again held the public trust. John Truman, father of Harry Truman, served as one of Jackson County's thirty-six road overseers, and Jack Reagan, father of Ronald Reagan, held a minor position in Franklin Roosevelt's work program.

The private strengths of the fathers of the presidents, rather than their worldly success, may have had the strongest influence on their sons. Although both John Truman and Jack Reagan held insignificant government offices, their strong devotion to their ideals is significant. John Truman, took politics very seriously. Around election time he often came home badly bruised from a fight with what he referred to as another "black-hearted Republican." Jack Reagan also showed strength of character. Once he stormed out of a hotel when he discovered that its management boasted that it did not take Jews as guests. Before leaving, Jack Reagan told the clerk, "I'm a Catholic, and if its come to the point where you won't take Jews, you won't take Catholics."

Both John Truman and Jack Reagan were also known for their sense of humor, a quality they evidently passed on to their sons. Harry Truman's father was known to knock people's hats off playfully in a crowd, a prank that delighted his children. Ronald Reagan's father was quick-witted and a natural storyteller. "Always the salesman, you'd be sure that Jack had a story that would leave you laughing," a Dixon, Illinois neighbor of Reagan's recalled. "I think his son acquired his gift for one-liners."

William Howard Taft's father was a model of kindness. This opinion of him was conveyed many times, although never quite as eloquently as when First Lady Nellie Taft said:

> My husband's father was gentle beyond anything I ever knew. He was a man of tremendous firmness of purpose and just as set in his views as any one well could be, but he was one of the most lovable men that ever lived because he had a wide tolerance and a strangely "understanding sympathy" for everybody. He had a great many friends and to know him was to know why this was so.

William H. Taft's reputation for kindness proved his father's influence.

The exception that perhaps proves the rule to the importance of principles, humor, and kindness, is Nixon's father. Frank Nixon provides a very different profile of a president's father. He seemed to be a staunch Democrat until Republican President William McKinley spotted Nixon in a parade and complimented him on the beautiful horse he was riding. Right after that incident, Frank Nixon shifted his allegiance to the Republicans. In later years, when someone pointed out the incident, Frank Nixon was not at all amused. He was not often amused about anything, in fact, and had difficulty appreciating the humorous side of life. He was basically an intense person with a belligerent manner and a terrible temper. A neighbor recalled that when Frank Nixon "yelled at the boys, everyone for blocks around could hear....His temper frightened people."

It may be, however, that neither the worldly success nor the private strengths of presidential fathers is as important as the simple and surprising fact that they have been on average thirty-five years old when the presidents were born; the role models the fathers provided, whether good or bad, were often older than most paternal role models. Only Rutherford B. Hayes and Andrew Jackson had no contact with their fathers, as their fathers had already died before they were born. And only ten presidents' fathers died before their sons reached the age of twenty-one. Most of them lived long enough to see their children through to maturity.

A Ford...

When Woodrow Wilson was president in 1913, Dorothy A. Gardner, daughter of Levi Addison Gardner, former mayor of Harvard, Illinois, gave birth to her first child. She named him Leslie King, Jr., after her husband. Dorothy was married to the boy's father for only three years. In 1915, Dorothy and Leslie King were divorced. Almost a year after their divorce, Dorothy married a paint salesman from Grand Rapids, Michigan.

For the sake of family unity, Dorothy's new husband adopted her three-year-old son. The boy's name was changed to his adopted father's name, Jerry. Dorothy never told her son about her previous marriage nor about his biological father. Between 1918 and 1927, she bore three more sons. Jerry had no reason to believe that the man he called father was actually his adoptive father. His adoptive father seemed to treat him no differently than he did his other three sons. Basically, all four brothers experienced an average childhood; that is, until a man arrived at the restaurant where sixteen-year-old Jerry was working. The man stood and stared, then approached him and said, "Leslie, I am your father." Young Jerry Ford was stunned; no one had ever called him by that name, and this man said he was actually his father. The two sat and talked briefly. They parted with no promise ever to see each other again. It was an enlightening experience for Jerry Ford and no doubt painful. Twelve years later, when Jerry was an assistant football coach and a law student at Yale, his biological father visited him briefly once again, but no other meetings ever came about. Ford never initiated any contact.

One of Ford's first actions as a congressman was to support a bill which made it easier for a woman to collect support for children of runaway husbands.

...and a Lincoln

In December of 1850, John D. Johnston wrote a letter to his stepbrother, Abraham Lincoln, in a final effort to convince him to visit Abe's dying father, Tom. Johnston had written similar letters to Abe previously, but they all went unanswered; Lincoln and his father had never gotten along. This time, however, Lincoln answered the letter. He said that he could not come and see his father. "My business is such that I can hardly leave now," he wrote. He also asked his stepbrother to tell his father that, "if we could meet now, it is doubtful whether it would not be more painful than pleasant."

Abe explained that he had not answered the other letters because it seemed to him that he could "write nothing which could do any good. . . . I sincerely hope Father may yet recovere his health," he continued, "But at all events tell him to remember to call upon, and confide in, our great and good, and merciful Maker, who will not turn away from him in any extremity." The letter was dated January 12, 1851. Five days after the letter was written, Thomas Lincoln was dead. He was buried on his farm in Coles County, Illinois. His only surviving, son, Abraham Lincoln, who lived eighty-five miles from his father, was not present at his funeral.

Both Gerald Ford and Abraham Lincoln issued executive orders granting amnesty to military deserters and draft evaders during their presidencies. Ford also granted a controversial pardon to former President Richard Nixon. Both Ford and Lincoln were known for their compassion in issuing pardons despite contrary public pressures. They both seemed kind and honorable, almost to the point of softness. Yet they both had found it so difficult to forgive their own fathers. Sometime between the deaths of their fathers and their rise to the presidency, they discovered that forgiveness is not a weakness but a strength.

After this president's marriage, he and his wife spent their honeymoon at his home and estate, the Hermitage. He had named it that before their nuptials. Unfortunately, his wife did not live to see him elected president. After serving two terms as president, he retired to his estate, where he died. He never remarried. Who was this president?

4

Brothers & Sisters

*It is easier to be the best in an average family
than it is to be the worst in a great family.*

—*Greek proverb*

Generals George Washington, Zachary Taylor, and
Dwight D. Eisenhower had something in common besides their rank. Something, in fact, that they shared with
over half of the presidents of the United States. They were
all middle children.

A surprising pattern emerges when the currently accepted birth order theory is applied to the presidents. The
term "birth order" refers to the order in which a person is
born in relation to his or her siblings. Birth order falls into
four categories: the only child, the oldest child, the middle
child, and the youngest child. Most researchers believe that
the only child has been given the most advantages in life
and will be the most successful. The oldest child in a family
is thought to be the next most advantaged, and thus has the
second best chance of being successful, with the youngest
child coming in third. In this scheme, the middle child is the
least advantaged with the least chance of success in later
life.

This theory may well hold true for most Americans,
but when it is applied to the thirty-nine men who became

president of the United States, the opposite seems to be true. According to the theory, an only child would be the most successful, so most presidents should have come from families with no brothers or sisters. The fact is that *no* president in the two-hundred-year history of this country has ever been an only child. The theory further contends that the middle child is the least advantaged, and consequently has the least chance of success in later life. Yet over half the presidents fall into this "disadvantaged" category.

Why do accepted beliefs not apply to these men and the office of president? Many middle-child presidents received extra doses of parental attention because of frail health or special talents. And sometimes the oldest child died and parental hopes were transferred to younger brothers. But for the most part, disadvantage in any form served to ignite, rather than extinguish, the aspirations of presidents-to-be. And the presidency, perhaps, requires a different set of abilities than most other high-achievement positions. It may call for those qualities that middle children are forced to learn early in order to get along with older and younger siblings—qualities such as diplomacy, teamwork, and compromise. Many presidents seem to have combined these skills with a remarkable persistence and will to overcome obstacles.

Presidents were influenced by relations with brothers and sisters alike, but little is usually said about their sisters. Presidents' sisters traditionally have not been either embarrassments or problems for the presidents. Usually, by the time their brothers had reached the White House, presidential sisters had blended successfully into the populace by assuming their husbands' surnames. In contrast, the last name of a presidential brother was a red flag to newspaper reporters every time he did something out of the ordinary. Presidential sisters usually received publicity only when their husbands tried to capitalize on their relationship to the president. Ulysses S. Grant, Warren G. Harding and, most recently, Jimmy Carter experienced such problems.

George Washington, Thomas Jefferson, Abraham Lincoln, Rutherford B. Hayes and Harry Truman all had close relationships with their sisters. The press sometimes reported that Harry Truman had two sisters and no brothers, when in fact he had one sister, Mary Jane, and one brother, Vivian, whose given name was actually John Vivian. His preference for using only his middle name and the practice of dressing young children in unisex gowns in the late 1800s might explain why so many publications were confused as to Vivian's sex. Vivian Truman was a dairy farmer for most of his life but was appointed Director of the Federal Housing Authority of Missouri and held that position before his retirement.

Vivian was one of many presidents' brothers to hold a position in government service. Milton Eisenhower was appointed by his brother to a fact-finding tour of Latin America during Ike's term in the White House. David McKinley probably had the nicest appointment; he was the United States consul general to Hawaii. Ulysses S. Grant came under fire in the press when he appointed his brother Orvil to run a lucrative United States Army PX. In those days, PX's were considered a type of concession and PX managers charged customers whatever they liked and kept the profits for themselves. Grant was further criticized for appointing his brother to at least four other lucrative and cushy jobs during his terms as president.

When Andrew Johnson became the seventeenth president of the United States, his brother William came to the White House seeking an appointed position. President Johnson, apparently alarmed at the prospect of William's taking up residence in Washington, D.C., appointed him United States marshal to the state of Texas and never heard from him again. John Quincy Adams's brother Thomas Boylston Adams was chief justice of the Massachusetts Supreme Court. President John F. Kennedy incurred a lot of criticism when he appointed his brother to the position of United States attorney general. Robert Kennedy had previously been a United States senator from the state of New York. Kennedy's youngest brother, Edward, was also elected to the United States Senate. The Kennedy's seem to hold the record for presidents' brothers in elected office. Several brothers of presidents served in the United States House of Representatives, including Carter Bassett Harrison (William Henry Harrison's brother), Charles Phelps Taft, and William H. Polk.

Billy Carter, brother of Jimmy Carter, tried his hand at politics in 1976 when he ran for mayor of Plains, Georgia. When he lost that election, he commented to the press, "I lost because of the Baptist vote, the black vote, and the white vote."

Many of these men were successful, but felt overshadowed by their president-brothers. Zachary Taylor and James Madison both had brothers who were generals, Joseph P. Taylor and William Madison. Two physicians, George Harding and Wat Henry Tyler, were the brothers of Presidents Warren G. Harding and John Tyler. James Buchanan and Grover Cleveland had brothers who were men of the cloth, the Reverend Edward Buchanan and the Reverend William Neal Cleveland.

Some presidential brothers found employment with the president himself. Joseph P. Monroe, brother of President James Monroe, was the president's personal secretary. Sam Houston Johnson, Lyndon Johnson's brother, started working for Lyndon right out of law school. He continued to work for Lyndon right into the White House but complained that his brother was a taskmaster. "Anyone who works for Lyndon deserves the Purple Heart," he once said. The pressures of politics, Lyndon's idiosyncrasies and, most of all, the pressure of living in the shadow of his dynamic brother caused Sam Houston to become dependent upon the bottle.

A startling number of presidents' brothers were alcoholics. George Washington's brother Charles was a constant concern to George because of his drinking problem. The Roosevelt family had an explanation for why Teddy's brother Elliott drank so much; they thought he might have had a brain tumor from childhood, and the constant pain created a dependence on alcohol. John Quincy Adams's brother Charles lost a great deal of money he had invested for his family, and this loss was said to be the cause, at least in part, of his alcoholism. He eventually died of cirrhosis of the liver.

President Jimmy Carter's brother, Billy, eventually recognized his dependence upon alcohol and spent some time drying out in a rehabilitation center. While Jimmy was president, brother Billy raised many eyebrows with his gusto for drinking beer. He even came out with his own brand of beer. Billy Beer was popular for a while, but customers eventually looked beyond the label and expected good-tasting beer. Even Billy's mother, Lillian, said that Billy Beer was "godawful."

Donald Nixon once thought that he had a way to cash in on his brother's name. When Richard Nixon was vice president in 1956, brother Donald established a fast food hamburger stand that featured "Nixon Burgers." This venture quickly floundered, and he found it necessary to borrow money from Howard Hughes. Critics soon began accusing Donald of using his influence and his brother's name to obtain loans. He was hard pressed with a rebuttal since it turned out that he had put up a vacant lot worth $13,000 as collateral against a $205,000 loan.

Like Billy Carter and Donald Nixon, Abner McKinley, brother of President William McKinley, was also an enterprising spirit. Among many other get-rich-quick schemes, he once tried to talk future Vice President Charles Gates Dawes into investing in a revolutionary new process whereby synthetic rubber could be produced very inexpensively. While explaining the process to the skeptical Dawes, he remarked that the mixture had to be left alone and in total darkness. At that point in the explanation Charles Gates Dawes interrupted Abner and with a knowing grin asked if that were the step when someone would sneak in and "put the rubber in." He obviously did not invest in Abner's scheme.

When Samuel Washington, George's brother, needed money, he would go to one of his brothers for a loan. When brother George believed he had asked for money once too often, George complained to another brother, Jack, "In God's name, how did my brother Samuel contrive to get himself so enormously in debt?" One of the reasons for Samuel's financial problems might have been his five marriages and innumerable children. George was so concerned with his brother's philanderings that he left specific instructions in his will to pay off Samuel's creditors rather than give Samuel the money directly.

Although many presidents used their achievements to assist their brothers, often the assistance flowed the other way too. A young Ronald Reagan helped his older brother Neil get into college. Neil returned the favor years later when, as vice-president of an advertising agency, he talked Ronald into picking up his sagging acting career by accepting a job as host of the "Death Valley Days" television show. Borax, the sponsor, just happened to be one of Neil's advertising clients.

Sam Houston Johnson proved invaluable as a critic and counselor throughout his brother Lyndon's second term. He often would tell the president how he felt about a speech when everyone else was afraid to criticize it. Robert Kennedy was said to be ruthless in his political dealings on behalf of his brother's election campaign. Had it not been for another senseless assassination, Robert Kennedy just might have been the first man in history to follow his brother into the White House. Charles Phelps Taft, brother of William H. Taft, proved to be an asset when his newspaper, the *Cincinnati Times-Star,* endorsed Presidential Candidate Taft. Charles was the editor and publisher of the paper.

A few presidential siblings found it easier to seek success in fields totally unrelated to politics. Horace Dutton Taft, another Taft brother, founded the famous Taft School. Teddy Roosevelt's sister, Corinne, a poet and author, founded the first Red Cross War Chapter.

As for the president, the propinquity of a sibling may have given him an important gauge for his own talents and abilities. The sibling was a kind of sparring partner. The problem with this kind of competition was that where there was a winner there also had to be a loser, no matter how close the contest or how narrow the margin between the contestants. Just as the brightest star dims the brilliance of the stars around it, the men who became president often unwittingly denied their own siblings any satisfaction in personal success. Many presidents' siblings excelled in their own right but felt they could not surpass the achievements of their brother, the president.

In many cases this problem stemmed from childhood. While most presidents were personally aggressive, creative, and somewhat independent, the majority were coddled and babied well past childhood. The additional attention was very likely at the expense of their siblings. Sam Houston Johnson was well aware of the fact that his mother favored Lyndon. The Nixon children realized that their mother considered Richard special. Billy Carter complained that his brother got all the breaks. The siblings' frustration often led to disappointment and disillusionment, and sometimes even to alcoholism.

Billy Carter may have been more cynical than sincere when he told a high school graduating class, "Remember one thing: if you want to become a success in life, have your brother elected president of the United States."

A President Defends his Brothers

John F. Kennedy's wit helped him more than once to deflect the critics' fire, and there were times that he used it to defend his brothers as well as himself. When he appointed his brother Robert to the position of United States attorney general he encountered criticism that Robert lacked the necessary experience for the job. In smooth Kennedy fashion, JFK responded, "I must say that I am somewhat surprised at the criticism about my appointing my brother to be attorney general. I don't see what's wrong with giving Bobby a little experience before he starts to practice law."

The president also defended his brother Teddy when *Time* magazine wrote that Teddy smiled "sardonically." John Kennedy quipped, "Bobby and I smile sardonically. Teddy will learn to smile sardonically in two or three years, but he doesn't know how yet."

The Nixon Wiretappings

Biographers of Richard Nixon have suggested that Richard became an overachiever after the death of his older brother, Harold, in an attempt to compensate for the family's loss. Many friends and relatives had felt that Harold was the brightest and wittiest of the Nixon boys, so it was logical that after his death, Richard would try to emulate him for his parents. But Richard may have emulated Harold more than he knew.

In the spring of 1927, while Richard was in his early teens, Harold was stricken with tuberculosis. Their mother, Hannah, took Harold to the Pinecrest medical community in Prescott, Arizona, where she and her son shared a cabin with three other tubercular youths. The climate in Prescott was believed to be perfect for anyone suffering from any type of lung problem, and a medical compound for persons suffering from lung diseases had been set up. The youthful patients lived in the compound just as they would in a hospital; they were under a physician's care and spent most of the day in pajamas and bathrobes. Their illnesses and confinement did not stop the teenaged patients from falling in love with each other, and Harold Nixon soon fell in love with Jessica Lynch. Jessie, however, was not sweet on Harold, but on one of Harold's cottage mates, Larry Easton. Harold became so jealous of the affection between the two young patients that he sneaked up into the attic of the cottage and wiretapped a phone conversation between Jessie and Larry. He listened to their entire exchange of intimate talk. The next day, in an effort to embarrass Jessie, he repeated everything he had heard on the wiretapped phone.

Former residents of the Pinecrest community remember the incident to this day, and it was a private joke among them during Watergate. Did those Nixon boys have wiretapping in the blood?

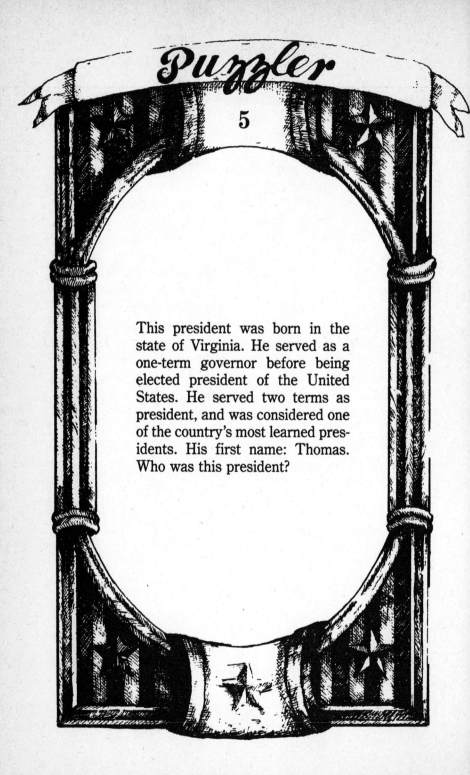

This president was born in the state of Virginia. He served as a one-term governor before being elected president of the United States. He served two terms as president, and was considered one of the country's most learned presidents. His first name: Thomas. Who was this president?

5

Names

I'm a Ford, not a Lincoln.

　　　　　　　　　　　　　　　—*Gerald R. Ford*

W hat's in a name? When it comes to the presidents, more than one might think. A rose may be a rose may be a rose, but sometimes a Washington may be a de Washington, or a Roosevelt a Van Rosenvelt.

Some interesting patterns emerge from a close look at the presidents' name. Though we tend to think of the presidents' last names as standard Anglo-Saxon names, many actually come from non-English names that the ancestors of the presidents Americanized when they came to this country. The first names of presidents were often those of their fathers, and their middle names were very often their mothers' maiden names, another indication, perhaps, of the influence these women had on their sons.

But whatever the names they had at birth, quite a few presidents decided to trade them in for something a little more exotic. Or at least acquire a catchy nickname. These men, who spent so much of their lives in the public eye, evidently knew that a lot rides on a name and, as usual, they wanted to stand out.

Well before George Washington's family even came

to America, it dropped the "de" from de Washington. When Hans Nicholas Eisenhauer came to this country, he Americanized his name to Eisenhower. Lyndon Johnson's family name was originally Johnston and Millard Fillmore's family switched over from Phillmore. Thomas Jefferson's name goes back many generations to the original Jeaffreson, and James K. Polk's name was originally Pollok. Herbert Hoover's great-grandfather Americanized both the spelling and the pronunciation of his name, Huber.

Franklin Delano Roosevelt might once have been Franklin De la Noye Van Rosenvelt. De la Noye became Delannoy became Delano. The Roosevelt name changed from Van Rosenvelt around the mid-1600s, and the pronunciation of the name has been an issue ever since. Elliot Roosevelt, Franklin's son, stated that the Hyde Park Roosevelts pronounced the name "Rose-uh-velt," while the Oyster Bay Roosevelts, Teddy's side of the family, pronounced the name "Rews-velt." One of Teddy Roosevelt's grandchildren, however, refuted Elliot's claim: "He's looney; we have always pronounced our name 'Rose-uh-velt'."

Ronald Reagan has no such problems with his name. "Those who called themselves 'Reegun' were the lawyers and doctors," said Reagan. "It was only the laborers and the farmers who called themselves 'Raygan'."

Some presidents' names go a long way back just as they are, with their own histories. The fame of President Benjamin Harrison's name goes back to the American Revolution, to his great-grandfather Benjamin Harrison who signed the Declaration of Independence. Calvin Coolidge's original first name, John, was the name of the first Coolidge to come to this country back in 1630. The name of John Adams can be traced back to President John Adams's great-great-great-great-great-grandfather, who lived in England around 1539.

Often, presidents got their names through just this

process of handing a name down from father to son. Besides John Adams and (John) Calvin Coolidge, Presidents James Madison, Andrew Jackson, John Tyler, James Buchanan, William McKinley, Theodore Roosevelt, (David) Dwight Eisenhower, Gerald Ford, and Jimmy Carter were all named after their fathers. Ford, in fact, was named twice after his father: first after his biological father, and then after his adopted father.

James Madison and Zachary Taylor both owe their names to the same man. Their great-grandfather James Taylor, who was born in Virginia in 1673, gave half his name to one great-grandson and the other half to another.

Andrew Johnson was named after Andrew Jackson, who himself had not yet become president. Johnson was born in 1808 in a small cottage on the grounds of Casso's Inn in Raleigh, North Carolina. His father was the porter at the inn, and when word of the birth came everyone drank a toast to the baby boy and his parents. It was December 29, and the guests were already in a holiday mood. As the party rolled on, everyone started suggesting names for the baby. A group visiting from Tennessee suggested the name Andrew after a lawyer they all respected, Andrew Jackson. Little did anyone know just how appropriate the choice of names was; Jackson went on to the White House, followed ten presidents later by his namesake, Andrew Johnson.

It is not unusual for a mother's maiden name to be used as her child's middle name, but the custom is especially prevalent among the presidents. Their mothers, it seems, had a great deal of influence on them from the beginning. Lyndon Johnson was named after his father's friend W.C. Linden, but maternal influence held its own and Lyndon's mother changed the "i" to a "y" and the "e" to an "o". Lyndon's middle name, Baines, was his mother's maiden name. Rutherford Birchard Hayes, John Fitzgerald Kennedy, Richard Milhous Nixon, James Knox Polk,

Ronald Wilson Reagan, Franklin Delano Roosevelt, and Thomas Woodrow Wilson were also given their mothers' maiden names as middle names. Ulysses S. Grant was named Hiram Ulysses at birth, but later changed his name, taking his mother's maiden name, Simpson, as his middle name.

Ulysses is, and was, a highly unusual name, and Grant's choice says a lot about how he, and the other presidents who changed their names, saw themselves. A number of them replaced their relatively common first names with their uncommon middle names: from Thomas Woodrow Wilson to Woodrow, from John Calvin Coolidge to Calvin, from David Dwight Eisenhower to Dwight, from Stephen Grover Cleveland to Grover, and even from Hiram Ulysses to Ulysses Simpson. It seems they all wanted to say "Look at me—I am someone extraordinary."

Changing their names also shows a shrewd understanding on the part of these men of the importance of a name in public life. Many who kept their names intact encouraged the addition of a nickname, knowing that a nickname could convey a particular personality. Jimmy Carter worked hard to ensure that his name appeared legally on the ballot as "Jimmy," rather than James Earl. Woodrow Wilson was delighted when he overheard someone calling him "Woody," and James Madison's friends all knew him as "Jemmy." But other presidents fought against the nicknames that the press had pinned on them; they did not like the image that the monikers conveyed. Theodore Roosevelt rebelled against "Teddy," and Ida Eisenhower was appalled when she heard someone refer to her son as "Ike." No one ever called Richard Nixon "Dick"—at least not to his face. "Well, I never called him Dick," Nixon's mother said. "He just seems like a Richard to me. Doesn't he to you?"

It was important to the presidents to have just the right name and many of them had no qualms about improving upon the one they had. Their willingness to do so is an indication of the unusual degree of self-confidence many of them possessed. They wanted the world to know that they were anything but common.

How Quickly We Forget

On March 4, 1933, after four years in office, Herbert Hoover became former-President Hoover. What had begun as one of the most promising presidencies had ended in near ruins. In 1928, Hoover was the golden boy of American politics. A young Franklin Roosevelt had called him "a wonder...I wish we could make him president of the United States." But by 1932, Roosevelt easily beat Hoover in Hoover's bid for a second term. The Great Depression had hit just eight months after Hoover started his first and only term in office, and he was blamed for the country's economic ills. He left office a fallen hero.

Hoover soon found out that, whether he was a hero or a villain, fame was fleeting. Shortly after he left office, he was approached by a young boy who asked for his autograph. When Hoover complied, the boy looked down at the paper, then asked for another autograph. "Why would you want two of my autographs?" asked Hoover. The boy responded matter-of-factly, "It takes two of yours in trade to get one of Babe Ruth's."

Not everyone even recognized the former president. When Herbert and his wife, Lou Henry, vacationed at a small resort in Canada, the excited desk clerk had their reservations waiting in his hand. As Hoover signed the register, the clerk could no longer contain his excitement. He asked Hoover if he were not related to ex-G-Man J. Edgar Hoover. When the ex-president said that he was not, the clerk was disappointed, but his face lit up again a few seconds later. He asked Hoover if perhaps he were a relative of the Hoover of Hoover vacuum cleaners. Once again the president had to disappoint him. The clerk sighed, "Oh well, no harm done. We do get a kick, though, out of entertaining relatives of real celebrities!"

Simply Harry

Rutherford B. Hayes. Grover Cleveland. Theodore Roosevelt. Ulysses S. Grant. Franklin Delano Roosevelt. In the company of such grandiose names, the name of Harry S Truman sounds comfortingly down-to-earth and simple. And in fact, Harry's name is what it is—not a nickname for anything more distinguished. But Harry came perilously close to being Harrison Shippe Truman.

John and Martha Truman wanted to name their son after his Uncle Harrison, but realized that everyone would end up calling him Harry for short. In no-nonsense Midwestern fashion, they made it easier for everyone by just naming him Harry to begin with. As for Harry's middle name, one grandfather insisted that it be Solomon, after himself, and the other grandfather favored Shippe, after his great-grandfather. A family crisis was averted when Harry's parents decided to make Harry's middle name merely the letter "S", thus allowing both grandfathers to believe that it stood for what they wanted. A most politic solution. Therefore, a period should not appear after Harry's middle name; the "S" is not an initial, it is his name.

JFK Loses a Prejudice

John F. Kennedy ran for office as a liberal Democrat. He won the support of many minority groups, and once in office was a proponent of civil rights actions. But he, too,

48

was subject to certain prejudices of which he may not have
been aware. When he was president, his aides would often
brief him on the next day's visitors. If the future visitor
were a person named Washington, Roosevelt, or any other
name of a former president, Kennedy was known to ask,
"Is he black?" One day, during a routine briefing, one of
Kennedy's aides told him about a man named John Kennedy. Before the president could say a word, the aide piped
up, "No, he isn't black."

Roosevelt Leverage

A famous name is a powerful thing, as Franklin
Roosevelt, John Quincy Adams, and Benjamin Harrison all
knew. Unlike Jimmy Carter who ran for office to refrains of
"Jimmy who?," these men benefited from the credibility
that their names inspired. But a respected name has its disadvantages too, as one Roosevelt learned in his dealings
with the shrewd Joseph Kennedy.

Kennedy, then ambassador to Great Britain, was interested in obtaining contracts with distilleries in Great
Britain, just before the end of Prohibition. But the English
distilleries were wary of illegal dealings, and Joe Kennedy
needed to reassure them somehow. He went to James
Roosevelt, Franklin Roosevelt's son, and offered to include
him in the venture. Roosevelt agreed and so did the English
distilleries; the name Roosevelt was magic. Joe Kennedy
then imported as much whiskey as he could into the United
States under the label "for medicinal purposes only." Joe
Kennedy made millions.

And what about James Roosevelt, who had helped
him obtain the contracts, and whose name had lent a sense
of security to the whole affair? Roosevelt received payment
for his help, but had expected a partnership or some kind of

share in the enterprise. When he approached Kennedy about his share, Kennedy laughed, and said that a Roosevelt could not make money off of liquor. "It would embarrass your father," he asserted.

A Trip Across the George Hartburn Bridge

How did one man's change of address in the year 1180 influence the future of the United States of America? When Sir William de Hartburn moved from his home of Hartburn, in the parish of Stockton, to the manor of Washington, the custom of the times dictated that he change his name as well. Instead of de Hartburn (of Hartburn), Sir William became de Washington (of Washington). Eighteen generations after the move the name would become the First Name of the United States, when Sir William's descendant General George Washington became the country's first elected president. Had Sir William not moved from Hartburn to Washington, the capital of the United States just might be Hartburn, D.C., and people all over America would be eating Hartburn State Apples.

This former Republican president was shot in an assassination attempt while leaving his hotel. Although he was pale and bleeding, with a bullet lodged in his chest, he was in fairly good humor on the way to the hospital. He survived with little or no ill effect. There was much public outcry, however, when his assailant, whose first name was John, was declared insane instead of being convicted of attempted murder. Who was this president?

6

Prophecies

*What's the sense of being born in the upper class
if you can get killed like the lower class?*

—*King Arthur in* Camelot,
JFK's favorite musical

When Grover Cleveland was president, he shook the hand of the son of a New York railroad executive and said, "I'm going to make a strange wish for you, little man....I wish for you that you may never be president of the United States." The boy, no more than seven years old at the time, was young Franklin Delano Roosevelt. Such "stranger than fiction" connections between presidents have always delighted the reporters and biographers who uncover them. Did Cleveland catch a glimpse of presidential destiny in young Franklin Roosevelt? Or did Cleveland greet all small boys this way, intoning the burdens of office and his own grandeur in not wishing it upon others?

Consider this thread of presidential coincidence: when Thomas Jefferson was a student at William and Mary College, his roommate was John Tyler, who was to be the father of the president of the same name. In his turn, the younger John Tyler and John Quincy Adams often met to play cards at a third friend's house. This card-playing friend was one-term Congressman James J. Roosevelt, great uncle of Teddy Roosevelt and cousin of Franklin Delano

53

Roosevelt. Skeptics may point out that such instances are not *so* astounding in a young country with a small population, only a handful of universities, and a limited circle of men in public life. But take a look at a twentieth-century version of the story. The scene is Kansas City, Missouri. Two young men who live in the same boarding house and work together at the National Bank of Kansas City strike up a friendship. One is twenty-year-old Harry Truman. The other is Arthur Eisenhower, older brother of Dwight D. Eisenhower.

The most famous coincidences and prophecies surround presidential deaths. For example, Thomas Jefferson and John Adams died on the same day—July 4, 1826—exactly fifty years after the Declaration of Independence. Adams's last words were, "Jefferson lives...." School children have relished the sparks of destiny and portent in this story for more than a century. Premonitions of death are another theme in presidential biographies. After John Tyler had left office, Julia Tyler had a vivid dream that her husband had died while he was away from home on business. She was so alarmed that she hurried to Richmond, and arrived to find her husband recovering from an illness he had come down with two days before. He appeared to be in good health. Mrs. Tyler's relief was shortlived, however. Tyler's health collapsed again two days later, and he died of "bilious fever."

A great deal of uncanny lore surrounds the death of Abraham Lincoln. Shortly before his assassination, Lincoln had a dream. In the dream he awoke and walked through an almost eerie, silent White House. When he heard the sounds of sobbing, he followed them to the East Room and discovered a draped coffin. Lincoln asked one of the military guards standing by the coffin, "Who is dead?" The guard replied, "The president." Lincoln was so shaken by the immediacy of the dream that he described it to his aides and even discussed it later in a cabinet meeting.

James Garfield, the next president to be assassinated, also seemed to experience a premonition of his own death. History tells us that he summoned Robert Lincoln, son of the late president, to the White House for a private meeting. When Lincoln arrived, Garfield questioned him about his father's death. Robert Lincoln answered the president's questions for about an hour, recalling details of his father's assassination. Two days later, Garfield himself was assassinated.

The strange constellation of facts surrounding Lincoln's death includes one final story. On April 25, 1865, a photograph was taken of Lincoln's funeral procession going down Broadway in New York City. The faces of two young boys are seen on the second floor of the home of their grandfather, C.V.S. Roosevelt. The boys are future president Theodore Roosevelt, age six, and his younger brother Elliott, future father of Eleanor Roosevelt.

The Mary Todd Prophecy

No summary of the signposts pointing to Abraham Lincoln's destiny is complete without the tale of Mary Todd Lincoln and her suitors. Young Mary Todd was the daughter of a wealthy Kentucky lawyer, politician and businessman. She was only eight years old when her mother died, so Mary Todd was brought up by an aunt. At the age of twenty-one, she went to live with her sister Elizabeth Todd Edwards in Springfield, Illinois. Elizabeth was married to the son of the governor of that state, so it was little wonder that Mary quickly was able to meet some of the leaders of Illinois society.

Blue-eyed Mary Todd was radiantly beautiful. She had long dark lashes, lovely brown hair, and a pretty, dimpled smile. In just a short time she became one of the most popular and eligible young ladies in Springfield. She was courted by some of Illinois' brightest young bachelors. When her sister once asked her whom she intended to marry, Mary Todd answered, "The one that has the best chance of becoming president." That statement and her eventual decision become even more amazing considering her options.

When she expressed her prophetic preference, she was seeing both Stephen A. Douglas and Abraham Lincoln, among other suitors. Douglas must have appeared to have far greater prospects of becoming president than the struggling and impoverished Abraham Lincoln. Yet Mary Todd went ahead and married Abraham Lincoln while he was still an obscure state legislator. At the same time Stephen A. Douglas was already a prominent national political figure.

The rest, as they say, is history. Douglas went on to become United States senator from Illinois. He ran for re-election against Abe Lincoln. Although Lincoln lost that election and Douglas retained his Senate seat, the Lincoln-Douglas Debates brought Abe Lincoln to national prominence. Almost a full twenty years after Mary Todd announced her prophecy to her sister, her husband, Abraham Lincoln, became the sixteenth president of the United States by finally defeating Stephen A. Douglas in *that* election.

A Prophetic Association

In September of 1862, while Abraham Lincoln sat in the White House wrestling with the problems of the Civil War, on the battlefield a nineteen-year-old mess sergeant named Billy risked his own life to bring food to war-weary troops on the firing line. Hours before, their colonel had ordered the men back to the front without allowing them to eat. Billy, concerned about their welfare, immediately prepared sandwiches with the remaining beef and bread available. Then, without consulting the colonel, he ran along the firing line and dodged bullets, passing out sandwiches to the grateful troops. After he completed his mission, the troops rang out with a joyous cheer, and with renewed spirit and strength, continued the battle.

As soon as the colonel learned about Billy's display of courage and compassion, he promoted Billy to second lieutenant. The incident might have gone unreported to this day had the two people involved not become such important figures in American history. The colonel quickly rose to the rank of major general and, after the war, served in the House of Representatives. He was three times elected governor of Ohio and in 1877 became the nineteenth president of the United States. His name was Rutherford B. Hayes. Billy, his mess sergeant, eventually became an Army major and, after the war, he too served in the United States House of Representatives. After serving two terms as governor of Ohio, he was elected twenty-fifth president of the United States. His name was William McKinley.

In Teddy's Footsteps: FDR and the Zero Factor

Sometimes Presidents seem to have consciously manufactured their own "fates." We know that many of them imagined themselves in office very early in life and seemed strangely "driven" toward their goals. Even Woodrow Wilson, who seemed destined for the world of academia, once as a college student tried on a political identity. He wrote jokingly on his calling cards, "Thomas Woodrow Wilson, Senator from Virginia."

Franklin Delano Roosevelt seems to have been, of all the presidents, the most conscious of parallels and patterns as he mapped out his career. As a twenty-six-year-old junior law clerk, FDR told his friend Grenville Clark that he was not going to practice law for the rest of his life. Instead, he planned to pursue a political career. In fact, he declared, he had a very good chance to become president.

As FDR explained it, he planned first to win a seat in the New York state senate, just as his famous cousin Teddy Roosevelt had done. He then hoped to secure a position as assistant secretary of the Navy, again just as Teddy had done. From there he would go on to the New York governorship, still trailing Teddy's footsteps. FDR was quoted as saying, "Anyone who is governor of New York has a good chance to be president with any luck."

But Teddy Roosevelt's rise to the presidency was peculiar in one respect; he was elected to the vice presidency during a *zero factor* year. The concept of the *zero factor* is well known to presidential buffs. Part numerology, part historical oddity, part jinx, it states that every president since William Henry Harrison who was elected to office in a year ending in zero never left office alive. FDR may have recognized the pattern: 1840—Harrison; 1860—Lincoln; 1880—Garfield; 1900—McKinley.

When McKinley died in office, Teddy Roosevelt became president. If FDR was indeed serious abut pursuing the presidency in exactly the same manner as his cousin, he too should have become vice president in a zero factor year and then become president upon the death of the president. This is exactly what he tried to do. He ran for vice president as the running mate of James Cox of Ohio against Warren G. Harding and Calvin Coolidge in 1920, a zero factor year. Although Roosevelt campaigned vigorously, visiting almost every state, Harding and Coolidge won by a landslide. Sure enough, the zero factor struck again; Harding died in office after only two years, and Calvin Coolidge became president.

Shortly after losing as Cox's running mate, Franklin

Roosevelt was struck by polio and lost the use of both his legs. He practically disappeared from politics from 1921 until 1928. Then, through careful calculation, he reappeared in the political arena. He gave a very impressive nominating speech for New York Governor Al Smith at the Democratic National Convention. Al Smith won the presidential nomination, but lost the election to Herbert Hoover. The strategy on FDR's part was twofold. First, he had succeeded in giving a very impressive nominating speech that was covered by every major newspaper across the country. He thus brought himself back into the national limelight overnight. Second, in helping to secure the Democratic presidential nomination for Al Smith, he assured the availability of the vacated governor's office for himself. He won it easily, moving another step toward the presidency along the route he had described years earlier to Grenville Clark. Once in Albany, he dazzled even the most skeptical of critics. He began to sound and act like a leader of the Democratic Party. After two impressive years as governor, he was nominated for the presidency at the 1932 Democratic Convention in Chicago. He won the election and was inaugurated the thirty-second president of the United States March 4, 1933.

And what of the zero factor from here? Of course, FDR himself was reelected for a third term in 1940, and did indeed die in office during his fourth term, in 1945. Chillingly, John F. Kennedy was the man elected in 1960. Those who like to cultivate the mystery of the jinx point out that Ronald Reagan, the man elected in 1980, might well have died from his gunshot wounds in 1981 were it not for modern emergency room techniques. His recovery may have put the jinx to rest.

This president was a congressman from Massachusetts for seventeen years. He was a one-term president, born in Massachusetts, whose first name was John. He was attending Harvard University while his father was representing the United States to the Court of St. James in Great Britain. While traveling through Europe with his father, he acted as his secretary. This president also represented the state of Massachusetts in the U.S. Senate. Who was he?

7

Education

What good is it to teach someone all the facts if they don't know how to live and if they don't know the use of them for the solutions of the problems they are going to meet as life goes on?

—*Ronald Reagan*

With the exception of Woodrow Wilson, the presidents of the United States have not been long on formal education. Generally it is their advisors, not they, who possess the top academic credentials. What's more, there seems to be little correlation between a man's performance in school and his performance once in the Oval Office. William Howard Taft, a disappointment to many as president, although a superb chief justice, was second in his class at Yale University. Thomas Jefferson, on the other hand, was a college dropout, as were James Monroe, William Henry Harrison, and William McKinley. President James Buchanan was expelled from college for disorderly conduct, but was later reinstated when he promised to keep on his best behavior. At least eight presidents never attended college at all. Three of those—Zachary Taylor, Abraham Lincoln and Andrew Johnson—had no formal schooling.

Of the thirty or so presidents who did go to college, many followed the gentlemanly tradition of attending the same schools their fathers did. William Howard Taft attended Yale, as did his father, Alphonso Taft. John Quincy Adams, Franklin Roosevelt, and John F. Kennedy were all Harvard University legacies. John Tyler attended William and Mary College, the same school that his father had attended with classmate Thomas Jefferson. Grover Cleveland's father, the Reverend Richard Cleveland, graduated with honors from Yale and did his religious training at Princeton, but since the pulpit is not a place for material success, Grover's parents could not afford to send him to college at all. After retiring from the presidency, however, Grover Cleveland was appointed a member of the Board of Trustees at Princeton University. Woodrow Wilson's father, like Grover Cleveland's, did his religious training at Princeton. Woodrow attended Princeton too, and went on to serve as its president from 1902 until 1910.

The favorite profession among our presidents has been the law; at least 25 former heads of state earned their livings as lawyers and/or judges. But of these only four actually graduated from law school: Rutherford B. Hayes (Harvard), William Howard Taft (Cincinnati), Richard Nixon (Duke), and Gerald Ford (Yale). Six other former presidents—William McKinley, Woodrow Wilson, Theodore and Franklin Roosevelt, Harry S Truman, and Lyndon Johnson—were law school dropouts. Only a few presidents earned masters degrees, and only one, Woodrow Wilson, earned his PhD—in political science—before becoming president.

Beginning with George Washington, however, honorary degrees were conferred in abundance on United States presidents. At his death Washington possessed honorary Doctor of Law degrees from Harvard, Yale, the University of Pennsylvania, Brown University and numerous other institutions including one from his namesake, Washington University. John Quincy Adams complained bitterly when Harvard University, his alma mater, conferred an honorary degree on archrival Andrew Jackson. When President Millard Fillmore was offered the honorary degree of Doctor of Civil Law by prestigious Oxford University, he declined, stating, "I have not the advantage of a classical education and no man should, in my judgment, accept a degree he cannot read."

Ronald Reagan, on the other hand, accepted an honorary Doctor of Humane Letters degree from Eureka College, the same school where he had earned his bachelor's degree in economics as a member of the class of 1932. He later joked, referring to his unimpressive grades in college, "In cap and gown, I stood in this place to receive an honorary degree—a happening which only compounded an already heavy burden of guilt. I had always figured the first degree you gave me was honorary."

Further, our heads of state have traditionally filled positions of leadership in academia, either before or after their terms in office. George Washington and John Tyler were elected chancellors of William and Mary College. Millard Fillmore, who, like Washington, never attended college, was elected chancellor of Buffalo University. Thomas Jefferson not only drafted the bill for the establishment of the University of Virginia, but also designed its buildings and supervised their construction. Along with James Madison and James Monroe, Jefferson sat on the Board of the University. Another Virginia-born president, William Henry Harrison, is listed as co-founder of Vincennes University Junior College. James Buchanan had the distinction of being appointed the first president of the Board of Trustees of Franklin and Marshall College. In addition to Buchanan and Wilson (who served as Princeton's president), two other presidents sat in presidents' chairs at colleges: James A. Garfield was president of Hiram Eclectic Institute (now Hiram College), and Dwight D. Eisenhower was president of Columbia University, a post he held from 1948 to 1952, when he resigned to become president of the United States.

Apparently a formal education does not confer the kind of knowledge a president of the United States most needs, nor the kind that our citizenry most respects. Education or the lack of it seems to have little influence over the constituencies that vote in elections, or over the more august leaders in academia itself who elect or appoint their chancellors and presidents.

The Eisenhower Presidents

Before General Dwight D. Eisenhower became president of the United States, he served for five years as president of Columbia University. How did a general with no experience in academic administration get himself appointed to such a position? A rumor that circulated at Columbia for many years might provide an explanation.

The story goes that when the board of trustees of Columbia met to choose a new university president, the leading candidate was the president of Kansas State University. That was Milton S. Eisenhower, brother of General Dwight D. Eisenhower. A secretary was directed to write to Eisenhower informing him of Columbia's offer. But the secretary, hearing the name Eisenhower and thinking only of the general, sent the letter to Dwight, not Milton. By the time the error was discovered, the members of the board were too embarrassed to tell the general that he had been offered the position by mistake.

Columbia officials adamantly deny this rumor. But is it possible that somebody at Columbia did make a mistake? After all, Milton Eisenhower was the Eisenhower in academic administration. All the presidents of Columbia before and after Dwight Eisenhower's tenure had experience in the field of education before accepting the president's chair. A Columbia University faculty member at the time of the Eisenhower appointment said:

64

When the rumor began to spread among the faculty that the new president of Columbia was going to be Eisenhower, we naturally assumed that it would be Milton Eisenhower. After all, we knew the general had no experience in college administration, and Milton already had quite a reputation. He was already president of a college in the Midwest. Imagine our surprise when the announcement was released and Dwight was our president and not Milton. . . . Shortly after the general became president of Columbia, Milton went on to become president of Penn State and then Johns Hopkins.

Milton thoroughly enjoyed the world of academia and relished every position he found himself in. Dwight, on the other hand, found his position with Columbia unexciting compared to leading our forces to victory in Europe. He was unaccustomed to the relative lack of discipline all around him, and he once referred to the student body and faculty as "a bunch of spoiled brats."

A former Columbia faculty member reflected on Eisenhower's appointment:

Later the scuttlebutt was that when the Eisenhower name came up during the meeting, the board of trustees actually believed, even momentarily, that they were talking about Milton, except for one board member. This member later took it upon himself to go to the general and offer him the position. Of course General Eisenhower's first reaction was, "You have the wrong Eisenhower; you want to talk to my brother, Milton." The board member persisted; Eisenhower finally accepted and the University was in the corner.

The Truman Influence

Harry S Truman had planned to go straight to college after high school. He knew that his family could not pay for his education; his father, John Truman, had lost everything in a business venture and barely made enough to support their household. Harry was determined to go to college all the same. His plan all along was to attend West Point and get "a good, free education." But his intentions were thwarted by two problems: his eyes were so bad that he needed thick glasses, and West Point, as a military academy, had vision requirements he could not meet; and, more importantly, his father became so ill that Harry and his brother, Vivian, had to go to work to support the family. They both got jobs at Kansas City banks. Eventually, Harry gave up his plans to attend West Point and moved into a boarding house run by a Mrs. Trow, where Arthur Eisenhower, a fellow employee at the bank, also happened to live. "Arthur Eisenhower and I got along very well indeed," Truman was later quoted as saying.

Dwight Eisenhower was barely a teenager when Harry and Arthur got to know each other. In 1910, when Dwight graduated from high school, Arthur and Harry had already gone their separate ways. The Eisenhowers, like the Trumans, were in tight straits financially, so Dwight and his brother Edgar tried to take turns helping each other through college. Dwight would work for a semester while Edgar went to school, and then Edgar would work for a semester while Dwight went to school. It did not take long to discover that this plan was unworkable; neither brother could expect to keep a well-paying job for only one semester, quit, and then find a similar job one semester later. Perhaps older brother Arthur had a suggestion at that time, an idea he had heard from an old friend at Mrs. Trow's boarding house. On June 4, 1911, Dwight D. Eisenhower entered West Point Military Academy. "It seemed to me that West

Point would be the best way for me to get a free education," he said. He graduated four years later.

It is most unlikely that the idea of going to "a school of war" was suggested by anyone in the Eisenhower home. The Eisenhowers belonged to a strict Protestant religious sect called the River Brethren, and brought up their children on daily prayers and Bible readings. The day Dwight left for West Point, his mother ran upstairs and wept in her room. She was deeply convinced that soldiering was a wicked business. The only thing she ever said to Dwight about West Point was, "It is your choice."

Was it coincidence or Harry Truman's influence via Arthur Eisenhower that prompted Dwight to apply to West Point? The early connection between these men makes it possible that Truman's hopes played some role in Eisenhower's later success.

The Fugitive President

When Andrew Johnson first met his wife, Eliza, he was an illiterate, runaway indentured servant. His father had died when Andrew was only three, and his mother supported the family by taking in washing and mending. She was unable to send her three sons to school, so when Andrew was twelve, he was apprenticed to a tailor as an indentured servant. Later, because of a childish prank (no one knows exactly what it was, except that it involved trying to get a young girl's attention), Andrew feared that he would be punished and so he ran away. For many years thereafter, Johnson was wanted by his master as a fugitive.

He eventually settled in Greeneville, Tennessee, where he set up shop as a tailor and met Eliza McCardle. In May of 1827 they were married by Magistrate Mordecai Lincoln, Abraham Lincoln's cousin. When they were married, Andrew Johnson could barely read and could not write at all. Eliza was a school teacher, and she took on the task of educating her husband.

Eventually Johnson's tailor shop became a place for townspeople to gather for stimulating conversation about local and national issues. Townspeople, in fact, were so impressed with Andrew Johnson that they elected him alderman of Greeneville. He rose steadily from then on to mayor, state representative, state senator, governor, United States senator, vice president and finally president. His rise from obscurity is perhaps the most touching and dramatic of all the stories of the presidents. He was a tailor by trade, but he became chief executive of the United States of America in spite of the fact that he had never in his life attended school.

He was one of two Quakers to become president. Both were Republicans. Although his wife and two children helped him immensely during his election campaign, it was his dog that was credited with saving his political career just before his presidential election. Who was this twentieth century president?

8

Pets

The fact that dogs haven't given up on humans completely and still make people their friends shows there must be some hope for the human race.

—*Lyndon B. Johnson*

Abraham Lincoln had a dog named Fido. Herbert Hoover let his son Allen keep two pet alligators in a White House bathtub. Most presidents of the United States have been animal lovers, but apparently most historians of the presidents have not. Very often a history text will describe a president weathering some crisis of state alone in his office, when in reality he was not alone at all—he was accompanied by his dog. At one point during the Cuban Missile Crisis, Kennedy was said to have spent forty-five minutes alone in the Oval Office before calling for his aides. But White House records show that during this interval he had the White House Dog Keeper bring him his dog Charlie. Lyndon Johnson called for his dog before he announced that he would not seek reelection. Franklin Roosevelt very often chose the company of his dog when he went into seclusion, as did presidents Lincoln, Harding, Coolidge, and Nixon. Richard Nixon once had his Irish setter King Timahoe brought into his hospital room during an illness.

Research has shown that caring for a pet significantly reduces stress, hypertension and heart disease. The ambi-

71

tious men who became president evidently needed an outlet for the stress of their demanding careers and many found relaxation with their pets.

Presidents depended on their pets not only in times of anxious solitude, but in happier times, too. Abe Lincoln used to sit on the floor and talk and play with his cats for hours at a stretch. Mrs. Lincoln sometimes told friends that cats were his hobby. And many times she had to shoo Abe, Fido, and the boys outside when they got carried away with their playing and knocked over the White House furniture. She was quite upset when Abe insisted on taking Tad's two pet goats in the carriage with them on their journey to the Old Soldiers Home, which was the presidential retreat in those days, much like Camp David today.

The White House grounds have seen many other animals come and go, including turkeys, raccoons, snakes, sheep and horses. Once when Archie Roosevelt, son of Theodore Roosevelt, was sick in bed with the measles, his brother Quentin smuggled Algonquin, Archie's horse, into his upstairs room for a visit.

Historians have missed some valuable lessons by ignoring presidential pets. Calvin Coolidge, for instance, provided us with a perfect lesson in leadership when, during his first month in office, he decided to make his initial cabinet meeting a breakfast meeting in the White House. All eyes were on Silent Cal when he poured his coffee into his cup. Everyone at the table did the same. Then the president poured some coffee from his cup into his saucer. Once again, all his cabinet members did the same. Then he proceeded to add sugar and cream to his saucer, being very careful to mix it thoroughly. Again, every did likewise. Then, as the president picked up his saucer and placed it on the floor for his cat, Tiger, to drink, he noticed from the corner of his eye all of his cabinet members drinking their coffee from their saucers. There are leaders, and there are followers.

Franklin Roosevelt's dog, Fala, became a symbol of the president's commitment to the war effort in World War II. Fala was the first dog to become an official U.S. Army private. Immediately hundreds of thousands of dog owners sent one dollar to the president toward the war effort and in return received an official U.S. Army private's commission for their own dogs. During World War I, Woodrow Wilson had sheep grazing on the White House lawn in a dual effort to provide material for bandages and to keep the lawn trimmed, thus eliminating the need for an employee who could be better utilized in a defense plant.

First Ladies generally shared their husbands' enthusiasm for their pets. When First Lady Nancy Reagan was asked by a reporter what she missed most about leaving home to live in the White House, she responded, "I miss my dogs." Grace Coolidge's official portrait, which hangs in the White House, includes the likeness of her dog. A 1932 White House Christmas card from Lou Henry Hoover contained pictures of her dogs. The card read, "Merry Christmas from Lou Henry, Pat and Weejie."

Andrew Jackson Gets the Last Word

Andrew Jackson was a notorious rowdy and a consummate survivor. At the age of fourteen he proved his manhood by fighting in the American Revolution. He lived through that war and others, as well as numerous duels, one in which he received a bullet just above the heart. He survived a bout with smallpox and an assassination attempt, the first against an American president. He was the commanding general in the greatest American victory in the War of 1812, the Battle of New Orleans. He was once described as an uneducated scoundrel whose only interests were drinking, gambling, and swearing. When Jackson received an honorary degree from Harvard University in 1833, former president and Harvard alumnus John Quincy Adams protested to the president of the university, "As myself an affectionate child of our alma mater, I would not be present to witness her disgrace in conferring the highest literary honors upon a barbarian who could not write a sentence of grammar and hardly could spell his own name."

Nicknamed Old Hickory for a wood as tough as he, Jackson rarely revealed his other side, that of devoted husband and loving father and grandfather. Jackson's letters to his wife, Rachel, were full of love and affection, and he was not afraid to exhibit his tenderness publicly. He said of Rachel, "Heaven will be no heaven for me if she is not there." When she died, Jackson looked after her parrot, Poor Poll, and became very attached to the bird. Even when affairs of state were overwhelming, he found the time to write home and inquire as to the health and welfare of Poor Poll. When his term of office ended and he returned home to the Hermitage, he had more time to spend with Poll, and his influence became more pronounced.

The extent and quality of that influence became obvious at Andrew Jackson's funeral. Before some three thousand dignitaries and mourners on the lawn of the Hermitage, the Reverend Doctor Edgar stood, preparing to read the burial service. Just as he was about to begin, the quiet was broken by a raucous stream of obscenities echoing from the gallery, where the general's favorite parrot stood on her favorite perch. Friend and foe alike recognized the language of the crusty old general himself. There was an awkward pause and no doubt many a suppressed chuckle as the bird and her perch were moved to a more remote location. Shortly thereafter the dedication resumed, and Andrew Jackson was buried alongside his wife, Rachel.

One of Jackson's lifelong friends described him as "one of the most roaring, rollicking, card playing, mischievous fellows and the head of the rowdies hereabouts." Even after his death, Poor Poll the parrot gave Old Hickory the last word.

The Johnson Dogs Were Part of the Family

Once, when en route to Camp David, two of Lyndon Johnson's aides expressed displeasure at having to ride in the limousine with the president's three dogs. They were shocked when Johnson immediately halted the motorcade and personally altered the seating arrangements. LBJ and his three dogs remained in the presidential limo; the aides were transferred to the secret service car behind them.

Johnson clashed with his own wife, Lady Bird, when he insisted that his dog Yuki be included in the official portraits of daughter Luci's wedding. Although the president lost the battle, he and Lady Bird were not on speaking terms for two days after.

Grant, The Tactician

When Ulysses S. Grant was eight years old, his father decided to educate him in questions of money management. Grant wanted a pony, so his father sent him on his own to negotiate the purchase, coaching his son on precisely what to say. The boy made his way to a neighboring farm, introduced himself to the farmer, was led to the ponies, and after examining and riding several of them, he made his choice. Then the negotiating began. "I'll give you twenty dollars for him," Grant began, "but if you won't take that, my father says to offer you twenty-five dollars and no more!"

After his election, as Grant was deciding what portions of his household to transfer to Washington, D.C., and what to leave behind, the matter of the family Newfoundland, Leo, arose. A man who remembered his lessons well, Grant offered the dog to his father for ten dollars. Grant, senior, countered with an offer of three dollars, and Grant, junior, accepted. The next morning at breakfast the new president looked out his window to find at least ten dogs tied to the trees in the back yard, howling and barking and making a terrific racket. Grant summoned his children and demanded to know what was going on. The children informed him that they were going to sell all the dogs to grandpa for three dollars apiece.

Laddie Boy, First Dog of the Land

Of the millions of dog lovers in the United States today, probably only a handful know the story of the presidential dog who, in two short years, charmed the country to such a degree that a monument was erected in his honor—the only First Dog to be so honored in our history. Shortly after Warren Harding assumed office, he received a small airedale puppy named Caswell Laddie Boy from Marshall Sheppey of Toledo, Ohio. Harding already had several dogs, but Laddie Boy soon became his and the country's favorite. The White House was swamped with gifts and letters addressed to Laddie Boy. The press had a field day when, on Laddie Boy's birthday, he and his canine friends feasted on a huge four-layer cake made of dog biscuits and covered with white icing. The dog who carried Washington, D.C. Dog License Number One became an international celebrity almost overnight.

The press revelled in Laddie Boy's daily rituals: fetching and delivering his master's newspapers, retrieving lost golf balls, even sitting in on official cabinet meetings, at which he had his own special chair. Like other members of the president's cabinet, Laddie Boy had political functions and the occasional parade to attend. On May 11, 1921, newspapers across the country featured a picture of Laddie Boy on top of his own float, leading the Be Kind To Animals parade.

In July of 1923 President Harding embarked on a goodwill tour of the western United States, and the newspapers featured their usual photos of Laddie Boy patiently waiting to hear the presidential motorcade on the White House drive, bringing his master back home.

But Warren Harding died on that trip west. When the funeral cortege arrived at the White House, Laddie Boy leapt with joy, but this time his enthusiastic welcome received no reply. Newspapers reported that Laddie Boy could not seem to comprehend his master's absence and the air of sadness within the walls of the Executive Mansion. His affection and loyalty touched the hearts of many Americans, among them a man named Louis Newman, of the Newsboys of America Association, who asked that every newsboy in the country contribute one penny toward a monument honoring the president's loyal friend, the most famous newspaper carrier of them all. Sculptor Basha Paeff designed and constructed the piece, and Laddie Boy contributed by sitting for it at least fifteen times. The finished memorial was presented to the Smithsonian Institution, where it now stands to commemorate the loyalty and devotion of millions of dogs all over the world, but especially the faithfulness of Laddie Boy, a dog who captured the hearts of the American people.

King Tut Saves the Day

By the time Herbert Hoover was ten years old, his father and mother were both dead and he had been sent to live with an aunt and uncle in Newberg, Oregon. There he attended business college and later graduated from Stanford University with a degree in engineering. By the time he was forty years old, he was a successful mining engineer and a millionaire. During and after World War I he gained a reputation as an efficient administrator as the chairman of the Commission for Relief in Belgium and later as United States Food Administrator. Because of his success in feeding the hungry of Europe, he was appointed Secretary of Commerce under Warren Harding and Calvin Coolidge. When Coolidge spoke his famous "I do not choose to run in '28," Herbert Hoover was ready to step in.

Unfortunately for his party, however, Hoover had a problem with his public image. He was generally described as "efficient" and "effective," never as "warm," "genial," or "compassionate." Many saw him as a calculating engineer, interested only in logic, statistics and reports. No one denied his abilities, but in order to receive his party's nomination he needed something to prove that he was an ordinary human, a "regular guy."

Hoover's campaign aides searched desperately for some symbol or token of his humanity that could change his public image. At last someone unearthed a photograph of Hoover with his arm around his dog, King Tut. Campaign aides worked around the clock to make sure that every newspaper and magazine in the nation received that photograph. That was all it took: when the country saw Herbert Hoover with his dog, the tide of opinion began to turn. Hoover won the Republican nomination and then the presidency—with the help of a Belgian police dog named King Tut.

This president was born in the heart of the Midwest and was the son of a poor farmer. Before becoming president, he and a friend had been partners in a retail business. The future president worked hard, but the business was a complete failure. Although he never attended law school, he went into politics. While serving as president of the United States, he was severely criticized because he fired a very popular Army general for failing to follow orders. Who was this wartime president?

9

Businesses

The business of America is business.

—Calvin Coolidge

Many a failed business man has found success as president of the United States. The nation's top job has gone to would-be entrepreneurs of every stripe, from swampland developer to the father of frozen orange juice.

While growing up, most presidents experienced first-hand the advantages and disadvantages of self-employment. Thirty of the thirty-nine presidential fathers were entrepreneurs. The spirit of independence and self-reliance they gave their ambitious sons did not always secure financial success, but it led to the White House.

Unlike John Kennedy and Theodore and Franklin Roosevelt, the sons of uncommonly rich and successful fathers, Martin Van Buren, Calvin Coolidge, Ulysses S. Grant and Richard Nixon sweated laboriously in their fathers' retail businesses before pursuing financial careers of their own. Ronald Reagan proved to be an exception. Passing up a chance to follow in his father's footsteps, as a shoe salesman, and someday own a shoe store himself, Reagan decided to take a less lucrative job as a radio announcer. He stands alone among presidents as a successful, professional entertainer.

Harry Truman held a variety of jobs and worked on his father's farm. In 1919, returning from the First World War, Truman went into partnership with Eddie Jacobson and opened the Truman-Jacobson Men's Haberdashery in Kansas City. At first the store did very well, but in 1922 the agricultural depression hit the Midwest. With most of their customers out of money, the haberdashery soon ran out of money, too, and went under. It took more than ten years for Truman to pay off the debts.

"We certainly have expected and ought to have our money," Andrew Jackson's creditors wrote, after his three stores and a tavern failed. In a daring move, Jackson rescued his reputation and recouped his losses in a horse race.

In 1940, a young Richard Nixon proved to be a visionary by starting a company called Citra-Frost and almost became the father of frozen orange juice. His idea was to produce and market the frozen juice and to do so he borrowed ten thousand dollars from a group of friends and investors.

"He worked like a dog," a long-time resident of Nixon's home town later recalled. "He was out there cutting oranges and squeezing oranges day and night. . . . They just couldn't make a success of it."

Nixon made one mistake; he froze the whole orange juice, not the concentrate. Years later, other companies would come along and make millions by marketing frozen orange juice from concentrate, which prevents unpleasant separation of the liquid and solid components. Unfortunately, Nixon lost every dime he had saved, in addition to his investors' money.

People who dealt with Honest Abe Lincoln fared a little better. In January 1833, after returning from the Black Hawk War, Lincoln and William F. Berry purchased a general store from the Herndon Brothers and opened the Lincoln and Berry General Store. Business was slow, so the partners obtained a liquor license and set Honest Abe up as bartender, making Lincoln one of the few presidents to serve in a bar before he served in Congress. When business still failed to pick up, the store just "winked out." It took more than ten years for Lincoln to pay off all the debts from that venture.

Not all presidents were failures in business. At the age of eighteen, Andrew Johnson opened shop as a tailor in Greeneville, Tennessee. Not only was his shop successful enough for him to live comfortably, it was his springboard to politics. The people of Greeneville chose their tailor to represent them as alderman. In later years, he was so proud of his skill as a tailor, he continued to practice his trade. When he was governor of Tennessee, he made a suit of clothes for the governor of Kentucky.

George Washington, who once formed a company to develop swampland, was a famous entrepreneur. Although that venture was not successful, when the father of our country died, he left a half-million dollar estate, which included vast land holdings.

Another successful businessman was Warren G. Harding, who at the age of nineteen became co-owner of the *Marion Star* newspaper in Marion, Ohio. He eventually became sole owner of the newspaper, buying out his two partners when he was just twenty-two years old. The *Marion Star* launched Harding's political career; the people of Marion chose their publisher to represent them in the Ohio state senate.

Herbert Hoover left millions of dollars after his death. He made most of his money in his engineering business. The son of a blacksmith, he had started in the business world by working seven nights a week for two dollars a night. While he was president, he donated his entire salary to charity.

Jimmy Carter postponed career plans to work the family farm. When Jimmy's father died at the age of fifty-nine, Jimmy left a promising Navy career in order to take over the family peanut business. Under Jimmy's direction, nuts grew into a multi-million dollar business for the Carters, proving Horace Greeley's axiom: "The best business you can go into you will find on your father's farm or in his workshop."

Although it may be impossible to judge what kind of president a person will be by studying how successful he or she was in business, the great failure rate among people who have gone on to become president suggests a strong resiliency and great determination. They have rebounded after defeat, showing an uncommon persistence level.

"Nothing takes the place of persistence," Calvin Coolidge once commented. Had Coolidge studied the men more closely who preceded him in office, he might have said, "persistence and risk." Financial success has not always characterized those who have held the highest office in the land, but the ones who failed in business persevered and did not fail to become president.

Two Sides to Every Counter

Abe Lincoln seemed to have been as honest with himself as he was with everyone else. He did not smoke or even chew tobacco. He never used foul language, even when he was upset. The worst language he used, as reported by his aides in the White House, was "By jingo!" Once when he worked in the general store and a roughneck refused to refrain from swearing in front of ladies, Lincoln dragged him outside and taught him a lesson in manners. Although it was widely known that he did dispense liquor in his general store, he refrained from drinking it himself. He was all too aware of the evils of alcohol; his partner in the Lincoln-Berry General Store lost his life to the bottle.

Ironically, Lincoln's political career was almost ruined when one of his opponents brought up the fact that Lincoln sold liquor in his general store. It was only because of Lincoln's quick thinking and sharp wit that he was able to kill the subject as an election issue. Abe responded that it was true he had sold liquor at his general store, but at least he was behind the counter. His opponent, he suggested, had been on the other side of it.

Haberdasher Truman

Exactly five months after Harry Truman and Bess Truman were married, Harry opened a haberdashery. His partner was Eddie Jacobson, a wartime buddy. The arrangement seemed to work well; Harry handled most of the selling, Eddie did the buying, and Bess did the books.

One day a woman walked into the store looking for a present for her husband. Harry suggested a nice pair of gloves. She agreed, but after examining all the gloves in stock, she told Truman that none of the styles were acceptable. Puzzled, Harry asked her exactly what kind of gloves she wanted. "After all," he said, "I've just shown you our complete stock of winter gloves." "Oh yes," the lady responded, "they are very nice, but you see they all have five fingers and my husband has six."

Bess Truman recalled another day when a man came into the store looking for what he called an "indoor umbrella." He explained that there was a leak in the ceiling of his bedroom, and every time it rained he got wet. Eventually Harry asked Bess to do the books at home because he did not want her to be subjected to some of the "strange people" who came to the store.

With more free time, Bess was able to read more of her favorite mystery novels. One day Harry returned home from work and noticed Bess reading a mystery novel that he had already read. Without thinking, Harry told Bess how the book ended. Bess was so upset with her husband for ruining the book for her that she told him she hoped all of his customers the next day would ask for six-fingered gloves.

Puzzler

10

This Republican president hails from California. He first met his wife when they were acting together. She played a small role in *The Black Tower*, in which he played the leading role. Before meeting the future president, she had appeared in such movies as *The Great Ziegfield*, starring William Powell, and *Small Town Girl*, starring Robert Taylor. Who was this First Couple?

10

Wives

No one can make you feel inferior without your consent.

—*Eleanor Roosevelt*

Martha Washington was usually addressed as Lady Washington. Her successors were known simply as "presidents' wives." It was not until 1877 that reporter Mary Clemer Ames, writing about the inauguration of President Rutherford B. Hayes, referred to Mrs. Hayes as the "First Lady." By 1911 the moniker was commonplace, as is evidenced by a hit comedy about Dolley Madison entitled "The First Lady of the Land."

Along with her title, the public image of the wife of the president has changed, along with the changes in the status of women in general. In the early days of United States history, it was not considered proper for presidents' wives or any other ladies to be public figures or meet officials at public ceremonies. As the status of women changed, the American public began to recognize the contributions of American women, and of First Ladies.

It is clear now that even during the earliest decades of our nation's history, most presidents' wives had direct influence over affairs of state. Abigail Adams was dubbed "Mrs. President" by one of John Adams's opponents who felt that she influenced Adams too much on political matters. Sarah Polk acted as confidential secretary to her husband, James, in what may have been the first partnership presidency. She alone chose what books and magazines the president would read, and she studied them herself, calling his attention to issues she judged important. She was known to be a good listener, with an excellent memory and a clear understanding of affairs of state. Polk often solicited her advice, and stated, "None but Sarah knew so intimately my private affairs."

As attitudes towards women changed, Sarah Polk saw the changes and rejoiced that it was "beautiful to see" women supporting themselves and gaining respect by it. Her successors' influence on the presidents was acknowledged more openly. Lucretia Garfield, Edith Wilson, Eleanor Roosevelt, and Rosalynn Carter, among others, were known to discuss affairs of state with their husbands.

Yet not all presidents confided in their wives on political matters. Grace Coolidge learned from a friend that her husband, Calvin, had announced to the press his intention not to seek reelection.

Beyond their influence on their husbands, First Ladies have traditionally wielded their own influence to further causes which they supported. Lou Henry Hoover was actively involved in the Girl Scouts of America, and conducted huge fundraisers for it. Mrs. Coolidge was committed to helping handicapped children at the Clarke School for the Deaf. Caroline Harrison, wife of Benjamin Harrison, combined fundraising talents with political action when, while helping to raise funds for Johns Hopkins Medical School, she insisted that it permit women to enroll. Julia Tyler became famous as one of the few female gunrunners during the War Between the States.

The interests of other First Ladies fell closer to home. Abigail Fillmore was instrumental in establishing the first White House Library. Helen Taft was responsible for securing three thousand cherry trees from Japan and having them planted in Washington's Potomac Park. She lived to see those cherry trees become an American institution. Dolley Madison began an American tradition when she initiated the first Easter egg roll on the White House lawn. She remains one of the most popular First Ladies ever; even after she left the White House she reigned over Washington society for over thirty-two years.

Only one First Lady ever served the United States government in an executive capacity. Eleanor Roosevelt was appointed to the United States delegation of the United Nations General Assembly by President Harry Truman. Her concern for human rights, her efforts on behalf of the victims of proverty, prejudice, and war, her strength in using her influence as First Lady to advance moral causes, and her dedication to her duties later as delegate to the United Nations, won her international respect and prompted President Truman to call her "the First Lady of the World."

Mrs. Monroe Returns a Favor

Presidents' wives have always embraced and furthered causes, but few have wielded their power as bravely and dramatically as did Elizabeth Monroe in 1794. When her husband was United States minister to France, she singlehandedly managed to save a woman from the guillotine.

The Monroes had arrived in France in May, 1794, one year after King Louis XVI had been sent to the guillotine. After the French Revolution, one group after another seized control of the unstable government and the guillotine was constantly employed beheading various political enemies and the aristocracy. It was a trying and bloody period in French history, and the Monroes stepped into the thick of it.

Not long after they arrived, they learned that Madame Lafayette, wife of General Lafayette, had been arrested and was being held in prison. Most likely she would be executed in a matter of days. General Lafayette had barely escaped with his life.

The Monroes were stunned. General Lafayette was a hero of the American Revolution. He had come to America during the beginning of the American Revolution, was quickly appointed Major General, and fought for the American cause of freedom at the Battle of Brandywine in Pennsylvania. After two years he had returned to France and persuaded the French government to send troops to assist the colonists. He then had returned to America and taken command of the Virginia Army. When, with the help of the French fleet, the American troops forced the British to surrender, the young and grateful nation hailed Lafayette as a hero.

James and Elizabeth Monroe did not forget their gratitude to Lafayette and were distressed at his wife's predicament. Although James Monroe, as a United States minister, could not interfere in the internal affairs of a foreign government, Elizabeth Monroe made her own plans to save the life of Madame Lafayette. In order to show the French government that America was interested in the safety and well-being of the woman, she paid a visit to the prison in her official carriage. She was accompanied only by her servants. Making sure that the guards took note of the seal of the United States on the carriage door, she demanded in impeccable French to see Madame Lafayette. The impressed guards did as she said.

A few days after Mrs. Monroe's visit to the prison, the French government released Madame Lafayette. Elizabeth Monroe's concern had saved her life.

Check and Mate

Mary Todd Lincoln was famous for her determination. One of Abe Lincoln's friends, Judge Treat, had occasion to see firsthand that she could not be put off when she had set her mind to something.

Abe and the judge both enjoyed chess, and were engrossed in a game one day in Lincoln's law office when one of the Lincoln children came in.

"Ma says its time for dinner, Pa," the child exclaimed.

"Tell Mother I'll be there directly," Abe replied.

His son left and Abe and the judge recommenced the game. As the minutes slipped by, the lawyer and the judge lost sight of the time, but they were reminded of Mrs. Lincoln's request by the boy's reappearance.

"Ma says to drop everything and come home to dinner now," he announced.

"Tell Mother I'll be right there," Lincoln responded calmly as the young messenger exited.

A long time passed before the boy made his third and final appearance. He had a look of determination on his face, obviously sent with special instructions from his mother. He said nothing but placed himself strategically near the chessboard. As Abe watched, his son swung his foot up and kicked over the chessboard, sending kings, queens, and bishops into the air and all over the floor. As if all chess games were supposed to end in that manner, Abraham Lincoln calmly rose and told the startled judge, "I reckon we'll have to finish this game some other time." And he walked home with his son.

First Lady, Mrs. Howard Johnson

All eyes were on Lady Bird Johnson as she and her entourage entered the Pennsylvania Howard Johnson's Restaurant. There were twenty-eight people in her party, including reporters, aides, and secret service men.

The waitress who took the First Lady's order seemed nervous at first, but recovered her bearing and served the group quickly. When they finished lunch and prepared to leave, a look of relief came over the waitress's face. An exiting reporter asked her how it felt to serve the First Lady of the land.

"The First Lady!" replied the shocked waitress, "Oh my God, thank goodness I didn't know she was the First Lady, because I would have fainted dead away. I thought she was Mrs. Howard Johnson, and that was bad enough."

President Kennedy's Other Wife?

When President John F. Kennedy was in office only eight months, an amateur genealogist, thumbing through a book entitled *The Blauvelt Family Genealogy,* found something astonishing. On page 884, entry number 12,427 read:

> DURIE (KERR) MALCOLM... We have no birthdate. She was born Kerr but took the name of her stepfather. She first married Firmin Desloge, IV. They were divorced. Durie then married F. John Bersbach. They were divorced, and she married, third, John F. Kennedy, son of Joseph P. Kennedy, one time Ambassador to England. (There were no children of the second and third marriage. One child, Durie, by the first.)

She immediately took the information to the *Chicago Tribune,* and they refused to print it. Next she told the *Washington Post,* pointing out that the book was available at the Library of Congress (card number 56-10936) and at the Daughters of the American Revolution Library. News traveled fast, and before any newspaper published the story there was a long waiting list for the book at both libraries.

The Kennedy staff immediately went into high gear to avert what they felt could be a juicy scandal. Press Secretary Pierre Salinger sought out the author of the thousand page book, Louis Leon Blauvelt, but found that Blauvelt had died two years earlier and his son-in-law, William K. Smith, was the current keeper of the Blauvelt family records. Salinger and Smith examined all of the records on which Blauvelt had based his information. The author cited his sources as a letter from Howard Ira Durie of Woodcliff, New Jersey, and a newspaper clipping. Both of these items were then discovered missing from the files. Salinger urged Smith to sign an affidavit that stated, "There is no material in the files about the president marrrying Miss Malcolm."

Next, the Kennedy people found Durie Malcolm and had her, too, sign an affidavit stating that she "had never been married to John F. Kennedy." Immediately after the affidavit was obtained, Durie Malcolm's telephone was disconnected at "the customer's request." Anyone wanting to question Durie Malcolm would have to travel to Montecatini, Italy, where she suddenly decided to go on an extended vacation.

The first major publication to run the story was *Parade,* but only after the magazine received over twelve thousand inquiries from readers asking whether the story was true or not. After a quick call to the White House, *Parade* ran the story in its gossip column in the form of a letter asking whether the rumors were true, and followed by Salinger's statement which, he said, was straight from the president: a flat denial.

Two weeks later *Newsweek* ran the information and called it erroneous. Benjamin Bradlee, Washington Bureau Chief for *Newsweek* and a personal friend of Kennedy's, quoted an unidentified "Blauvelt in-law" that the story was "a colossal mistake."

The Blauvelt family members who did have names disagreed. James N. Blauvelt, president of the Association of Blauvelt Descendants, told the *New York Times,* "I am sure that Louis Blauvelt could not have put it [the report] in his book unless he was sure of the facts." Mrs. William K.

Smith, Blauvelt's daughter, told a reporter that her father was "meticulous in collecting and organizing his material."

As the rumors spread, hundreds of thousands of calls and letters reached the White House, asking whether the president was married before his marriage to Jacqueline. The answer was always, "We have an affidavit from the Blauvelt Family Association in New Jersey saying there is no material in the files about the president marrying Miss Malcolm." It was true that there was no information in the files; what the stock answer did not say was that it appeared that there had been information in those files, and that that information had disappeared.

Most likely we will never know if the Blauvelt book had its facts straight or not. It would not have been beyond the Kennedys' resources, however, to wipe out the whole affair without a trace.

There is evidence that JFK at least knew Durie Malcolm socially. A 1947 article in the *New York World Telegraph* reported that Massachusetts Congressman John F. Kennedy had been seen constantly in the company of the "beautiful and intelligent" Durie Malcolm Desloge, but noted the "tiny obstacle...that the Kennedy clan frowns on divorce." (Durie had been divorced twice.)

This "frown" might explain why, if Kennedy *had* been married to, and subsequently divorced from, Durie Malcolm, the Kennedys would be so eager to cover it up. Divorce, or even annullment, was unthinkable for a successful politician, especially an Irish Catholic one. One divorced man, Adlai Stevenson, had already lost his bid for the presidency. Not until Ronald Reagan, twenty years later, would the barrier be broken, and a divorced man be elected president.

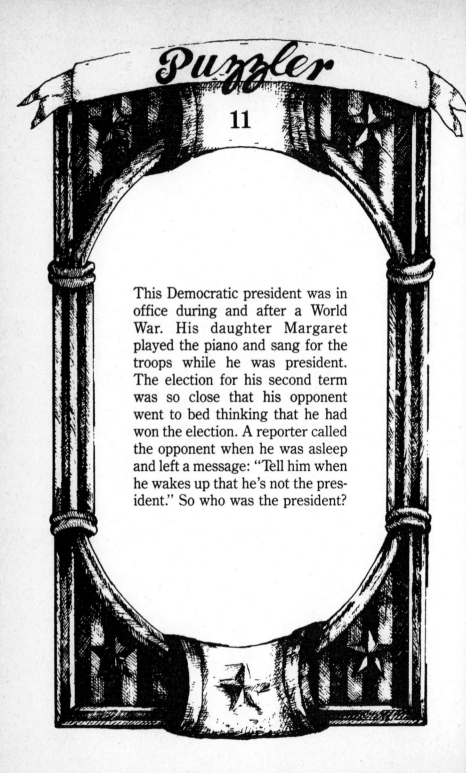

This Democratic president was in office during and after a World War. His daughter Margaret played the piano and sang for the troops while he was president. The election for his second term was so close that his opponent went to bed thinking that he had won the election. A reporter called the opponent when he was asleep and left a message: "Tell him when he wakes up that he's not the president." So who was the president?

11

Children And Descendants

One of the worst things in the world is being the child of a president. It's a terrible life they lead.

—Franklin D. Roosevelt

Shortly after Franklin D. Roosevelt was inaugurated as the thirty-second president, his youngest son, John, then a college student, came to visit him at the White House. He pulled up to the main gate of 1600 Pennsylvania Avenue in a typical college student's car, an old jalopy. The guards took one look at the car and turned him away; they were sure that no son of the president would be driving a car like that. John spent the night in a nearby Washington hotel, unable to get in touch with his parents. "I think the secret service expected the president's son to ride around in a chauffeur-driven Cadillac, whether he was a college student or not," John later recalled. "People just don't expect the child of a president to go to college and drive around in an old jalopy like everybody else."

Many people feel that extraordinary people must have extraordinary children. But no matter how accomplished or successful the children of the presidents may be, they are always compared to their extremely accomplished and successful fathers. Franklin Roosevelt's children, never considered very successful, would have been considered

99

great successes had their father been anyone else. Between the four Roosevelt sons, there were two congressmen, one mayor, one under secretary of commerce, one senior vice-president of a prestigious stock brokerage house, and one multi-millionaire in an import business. Still, John Roosevelt worried, "How could I do any better than my father? . . . . It would be impossible even to match him, but everybody thinks of everything I do in terms of my father."

John Eisenhower once said that being the son of a president "made it difficult for me to establish my own identity." The answer, for many presidents' children, was to play down their White House connection. Said John Coolidge, "I just wanted a normal life. I tried as much as possible to stay out of the limelight."

A son of Margaret Truman Daniel's heard from a friend that his grandfather had been president of the United States. When he asked his mother about it, she answered in the fine tradition of humble Harry Truman, "Yes, but anybody's grandfather can be president." Thomas Jefferson's five-great-grandson Jack Ruffin was once approached by his grandchildren who had just learned about their famous ancestor and wanted to know why their parents had not told them sooner. Mr. Ruffin replied, "We just didn't want you to think that you were better than anyone else."

Many presidents sent their children to public schools to keep them from feeling too different from other children. Often they insisted that their children work after school or in the summer like their friends. Calvin Coolidge, Jr., worked in a tobacco field one summer while his father was president, and an incredulous co-worker told him, "If my father was president of the United States, I would not be working in a tobacco field." Coolidge quickly replied, "If your father was Calvin Coolidge, you would."

That so many presidents' children did manage to lead fairly normal and successful lives suggests that presidents' children may be extraordinary after all. Even in the political arena, many managed to make a name for themselves. John Quincy Adams was the only son of a president who also reached the office himself. He also was minister to Great Britain, as were his father and his son, and was the only president's son ever to serve in both the Senate and the House.

John Scott Harrison, son of President William Henry Harrison, narrowly missed receiving the Whig Party's nomination for president in 1856. Twenty-seven years later, his own son Benjamin was nominated by his party, and went on to capture the presidency. Martin Van Buren's son John was asked to run for president on the Free Soil Ticket in 1848, but turned down the offer. His father, already the former president, accepted the candidacy, ran, and lost to Zachary Taylor.

Robert Todd Lincoln, son of President Abraham Lincoln, received several votes for the nomination at the Republican National Conventions of 1884 and 1888. He had been secretary of war under James A. Garfield and Chester A. Arthur. Lincoln came to believe that he was a jinx to the presidency after he was nearby during all three presidential assassinations of his lifetime: his father's, Garfield's, and McKinley's.

Robert Taft, son of William Howard Taft, was a leading contender for president more than once. As senator from Ohio, Taft received the second largest number of delegates' votes in the Republican National Conventions of 1940, 1948, and 1952. The first two times he was defeated by Thomas E. Dewey, who went on to lose the elections to Franklin D. Roosevelt and Harry Truman. In 1952 Robert Taft was defeated for the nomination by General Dwight D. Eisenhower, who captured the presidency.

Both Robert Taft and his son, the president's grandson, were senators from Ohio. Charles Francis Adams, son of John Quincy Adams; David Gardiner Tyler, son of John Tyler; and John Scott Harrison were also congressmen.

Franklin Roosevelt, Jr. was elected congressman from New York, and his brother James was a congressman from California. Both men however, lost their gubernatorial bids in those states.

In addition to Robert Lincoln, several other presidents' sons held cabinet positions. James Rudolph Garfield, son of James A. Garfield, was secretary of the interior under President Theodore Roosevelt; Herbert Hoover, Jr., was under secretary of state under Dwight D. Eisenhower; and Franklin D. Roosevelt, Jr., served as under secretary of commerce under Lyndon Baines Johnson. Charles Francis Adams was Lincoln's minister to the Court of St. James in Great Britain, and aided in keeping the British out of the War Between the States, despite Britain's need for Southern cotton.

Charles' son Charles Francis Adams, Jr., became president of the Union Pacific Railroad and a foe of Jay Gould. Although Charles, Jr., lost most of his investment in the railroad, his western real estate investments assured his status as a millionaire. Robert Todd Lincoln made a fortune in the railroad industry. He was a successful lawyer and later the president of the Pullman Company. Franklin D. Roosevelt, Jr., acquired wealth by importing Fiat automobiles into the United States. When his company, Roosevelt-Fiat Motors of America, became the national distributor of the cars, Fiat Company purchased his interest at a tidy profit for him. He then became a gentleman farmer like his father, and went into politics.

Teddy Roosevelt, Jr., attempted to reach the office of president using the same path as his father. He ran for New York State Assembly and won. Then he got himself appointed to the post of assistant secretary of the Navy, just as his father had done. He came up short, however, in his bid for the New York governor's mansion.

Teddy, Jr., did distinguish himself in a way his father would surely have envied. Theodore Roosevelt, Jr., became one of only two sons of United States presidents to be awarded the Congressional Medal of Honor. The medal was awarded posthumously for action during the Second World War in Normandy, France. James Webb Hayes, son of Rutherford B. Hayes, was the other president's son to receive the prestigious award, for action in the Philippines.

Two children of presidents followed in their fathers' footsteps and attended West Point: John Eisenhower and Jessie Root Grant. These two also distinguished themselves by writing books about their fathers.

A creative strain runs through the lives of many presidents' children and descendants. In addition to writing several books about her father, Margaret Truman Daniel has written mystery novels. Julie Nixon Eisenhower wrote a book about the people she met while her father was president, and her husband, David Eisenhower, wrote about his grandfather, President Dwight D. Eisenhower.

The most prolific writer of all the presidents' children or, for that matter, the presidents, is John Quincy Adams. He authored well over thirty books, including a complete collection of his own poetry. John Quincy was appointed Boylston Professor of Rhetoric at Harvard and was later elected to the Board of Overseers of the University.

Helen Herron Taft, daughter of William Howard Taft, became a dean at Bryn Mawr College and served for a time as the college's acting president. Harry Garfield, son of James A. Garfield, was a president of Williams College, where both he and his father had received their college educations. John Tyler's son Lyon Gardiner Tyler also served as president of his father's alma mater, William and Mary College, and was the editor of the William and Mary College Quarterly Historical Magazine. Lyon Tyler's daughter, Elizabeth, married Navy Captain Alfred Hart Miles, the composer of the song "Anchors Aweigh."

Because of their proximity to politics, many presidents' children married politicians, millionaires, or even nobility. President Zachary Taylor's daughter, Sara, married future President of the Confederacy Jefferson Davis, although Sara did not live to see the War Between the States. Ulysses S. Grant's granddaughter Julia became royalty when she married Prince Michael Cantacuzene, chief of staff to Grand Duke Nicholas of Russia, the commander-in-chief of the Russian Army. Julia probably met her husband when her father, Frederick Dent Grant, was United States minister to Austria-Hungary.

Theodore Roosevelt's daughter Alice married Speaker of the House Nicholas Longworth. One of the most famous of all presidents' children, Alice was barely seventeen years old when her father became president. Her uninhibited manner often shocked the polite society in which she grew up. Once she barged into her father's office when he was visiting with novelist Owen Wister. "Isn't there anything you can do to control Alice?" Wister asked the president. Roosevelt replied, "I can be president of the United States or I can tend to Alice . . . but I cannot do both." Alice continued to be a fixture in Washington for over eighty years, until her death in 1980, and she wrote a spicy book of memoirs about Washington society. She was best remembered for her caustic wit; in her living room she had a throw pillow with the slogan, "If you don't have anything nice to say about anybody, come sit by me."

Because Alice was Teddy's child by his first wife, who died shortly after Alice was born, Roosevelt set up a separate trust fund for Alice when she was an infant. When he suffered serious financial setbacks in 1887 he jokingly told his second wife, Edith, "Be nice to Alice; we might have to borrow money from her one day."

The advantages that go along with being the child of a president may obscure the personal successes and talents of many of these children. The bearers of famous names, they often became successes in their own right, coming to grips with the high expectations that the public and they themselves had set for them.

The Man Who Would Be King

If George Washington had become a monarch in the early days after the American Revolution, as many were urging him to do, it is likely that a mild-mannered engineer from Palo Alto would today be King of the United States.

There were certain factions within the leadership of the Revolution that advocated government by king, and the popular General George Washington seemed a good choice. Colonel Lewis Nicola of the Continental Army expressed the sentiments of others of his day when he wrote Washington that "the same abilities which have led us through difficulties apparently insurmountable by human power, to victory and glory, would be most likely to conduct and direct us in the smoother paths of peace...I believe strong arguments might be produced for admitting the title of KING."

Washington, however, replied, "Let me conjure you, then, if you have any regard for your Country, concern for yourself or for posterity, or respect for me, to banish these thoughts from your mind and never communicate, as from yourself or any one else, a sentiment of the like nature."

It is to Washington's credit that the idea of a king never got much farther, and that we have a president today instead. But had he accepted the offer and been successfully coronated, King Lawrence II might now be reigning as the sixth King of the United States.

King George would have reigned for only ten years before his death in 1799. The eldest son of the eldest son of Washington's brother Samuel would then have been next in line to assume the throne, as King John. King John's reign would have lasted forty-five years until 1841, at which time King Lawrence I would have been crowned. Fifteen years later, in 1856, King Daniel would have assumed the throne and guided the country through civil war. He would have been succeeded by King Thornton in 1887, and in 1935, at the age of thirty-four, King Lawrence II would have been crowned. Perhaps he would have received congratulations from Prime Minister Franklin Delano Roosevelt.

But because his great great great great uncle abhorred the idea of monarchy in the new country, Lawrence Washington's official title now is the much more modest Senior Representative of President George Washington. Born in 1899, the "man who would be king" is a graduate of the Massachusetts Institute of Technology and a Palo Alto resident who taught engineering at Stanford University. He and his wife live in a home they named "New Sulgrave" after Sulgrave Manor, the English home of the original Lawrence Washington back in 1510.

The "Trust Buster's" Son Stands Up to Big Business

When the Teapot Dome Scandal exploded after the death of Warren G. Harding, Archie Roosevelt emerged as one of its heroes. He would have made his father Teddy, "the Trust Buster," proud.

The scandal involved a number of former President Harding's cabinet members who had been filling their pockets by selling United States oil reserves to oil company "fat cats." These "fat cats" would in turn resell the reserves to the government at a hefty profit.

Archie Roosevelt had been working in a minor position at the Sinclair Oil Company when the affair came to light. He had overheard two company bigwigs discussing a payment of sixty-eight thousand dollars they were making to United States Secretary of the Interior Harry Fall. The senate was investigating improprieties in the actions of the Department of the Interior, and Roosevelt reported his information to Senate Investigation Committee Member Senator Thomas J. Walsh. When Walsh questioned the men Roosevelt had overheard, one offered the lame explanation that he had not said "sixty-eight thou," but rather "six to eight cow."

The findings of the senate investigation were enough to help topple Secretary Fall, the United States attorney general, and many who were connected with them. And Archie Roosevelt deserves some of the credit.

A Lesson in Horse Sense

Shortly after he graduated from Harvard University, Jimmy Roosevelt took "the grand tour" of Europe. He was traveling on limited funds, but his grandmother helped him out when he asked her. During the final leg of his trip, a fast-talking Irishman offered him a deal on a horse that the young Roosevelt could not pass up. The horse happened to cost exactly what the recent college graduate had in his pocket, and he was left without any money to get home. Jimmy sent his father, FDR, a telegram, telling him the good news and the bad news; he had bought the most marvelous horse, but he needed money for both himself and his newly acquired thoroughbred to get home. President Roosevelt sent his son the following reply: SO HAPPY ABOUT THE HORSE. SUGGEST YOU BOTH SWIM HOME. F.D.R. Jimmy got the money from his grandmother.

An illness in his youth once forced this man to leave college. After a successful stint in the military, he began his political career. As president, his popularity quickly rose after he successfully declared a naval blockade of Cuban ports. While in the White House, he also signed an act prohibiting the killing of seals in the North Pacific. This president had three brothers and five sisters. One of his brothers was a lawyer. The president died in office of wounds from an assassin's bullets. Who was this martyred president?

12

Health

Never throughout history has a man who lived a life of ease left a name worth remembering.

—*Theodore Roosevelt*

Health problems are a vivid and recurring theme in the lives of the presidents. A startling proportion of these men were frail, often housebound children. Others were stricken with serious illness in the prime of life. Of our thirty-nine presidents, nearly half have grappled with ill health and its frightening consequences.

Before he was thirty, George Washington had lived through smallpox, pleurisy, malaria, and dysentery: enough illness to kill off half a dozen men. James Madison, fragile and ailing throughout his youth, stood only five feet four inches tall when fully grown and never weighed much over one hundred pounds. But he lived well into his eighties, attributing his longevity to a lifelong exercise program. He never missed his daily walk no matter what the weather.

Like Madison, Rutherford B. Hayes and William McKinley were sickly children who spent much of their time indoors, reading. At nineteen, Woodrow Wilson spent an entire year indoors, reading and recuperating from illness. His studies paid off nicely; on their strength he entered and excelled at Princeton. John F. Kennedy was always sick as a child. His brother Robert once remarked, "When we were growing up together, we used to laugh about the risk a mosquito took in biting Jack—with some of his blood the mosquito was almost sure to die."

Harry Truman was healthy enough as a youngster, but his eyesight was so bad he had to wear glasses with lenses as thick as the bottoms of Coke bottles. He couldn't see well enough to play baseball and other boyhood sports, so he too spent his childhood reading, studying, and watching other children play. And like Madison, Truman as an adult believed that a daily brisk walk was a necessity to maintaining his health. He very often made reporters scurry along with him if they wanted to hear the answers to their questions—and he too lived well into his eighties.

Teddy Roosevelt, like Truman (and, incidentally, like Wilson), had terrible eyesight, but his biggest problem as a youngster was asthma, so severe that he led the life of a virtual invalid. His father sometimes spent whole nights carrying Teddy around the house in a desperate attempt to find a position or location in which the child could breathe a little easier. Teddy could not attend ordinary school and was educated by private tutors. The seclusion kept him frail and weak.

As he grew older his health improved somewhat, and eventually he was able to do a little travelling. Once, on a trip to Maine in a stagecoach, four boys riding with him began to tease him unmercifully. They roughed him up a bit, but the worst wound was to his pride. He vowed that he would never again let himself be humiliated by such an experience, and with his father's help and encouragement, he undertook a strenuous course of bodybuilding and exercise. Roosevelt, senior, had a complete gym built for his son in their New York home. Gradually TR, as he liked to be called, worked his slender, frail body into an impressive masculine physique. At eighteen, when he was ready to start college, he was a virtually perfect physical specimen.

110

For the rest of his life, Roosevelt pursued a course of strenuous exercise, and as president often required as much of reporters, carrying on press interviews in the midst of brisk hikes.

James K. Polk and Dwight D. Eisenhower suffered in their youths not from chronic poor health but from sudden, terrifying onslaughts of illness. An emergency gallstone operation, performed without anesthesia or antiseptics, brought Polk's schooling to an abrupt halt when he was seventeen. His long recuperation provided ample time to read and study, and by the time he was twenty he was able to pass the entrance requirements for the University of North Carolina.

An innocent skinned knee once jeopardized Dwight Eisenhower's very life. The wound became infected, and blood poisoning spread to the entire leg. When Ike learned that the doctors planned to amputate, he begged his brother Edgar to intervene. Edgar managed to forestall surgery; eventually the infection healed and Ike was able to enter West Point, the army, and finally the presidency.

Some presidents overcame their youthful ailments and lived far into healthy, productive old age. Others were less fortunate. John Kennedy's sickly childhood made him into an avid reader; later he, like Teddy Roosevelt, dedicated himself to the fit and strenuous life. But Kennedy encountered many setbacks in keeping to his physical goals. In 1954 a recurring back problem became so intense that he could not walk without crutches. He finally underwent two dangerous and painful spinal fusions. Undaunted by the surgery, he spent his recovery writing the Pulitzer Prize–winning *Profiles in Courage*. As president he kept himself fit, established the President's Council on Physical Fitness, and even demanded that his staff keep itself in good shape. He once noticed that many of his staff members were overweight and "flabby," so he asked everyone to lose five pounds.

Given Kennedy's poor health, imagine his reaction when he found that his vice president was more worried about health than he. Just before Kennedy assumed office, he had scheduled a goodwill trip to Mexico for himself and running mate LBJ. He wanted to demonstrate that his vice president would actually participate in executive duties. Johnson did not seem enthusiastic about the trip, however, and at the last minute one of his aides submitted a report predicting that the tour would result in major riots across Mexico. The Kennedy contingent was baffled; they felt that such riots were extremely unlikely. They soon found out that Johnson himself had requested this report. No one could fathom his reluctance to go to Mexico until George Reedy, a longtime Johnson advisor, wormed the truth out of him; LBJ had been afraid that he would get Montezuma's revenge in Mexico and then be too sick to attend his own inauguration!

Did their sickly, reclusive childhoods force our presidents into an early maturity? Did illness foster their ambitions, teach them determination and courage in the face of adversity? Certainly our presidents have shown more than ordinary fortitude in coming to grips with a more than ordinary share of physical affliction. Their personal histories have been profoundly shaped by illness, and perhaps our national history has been so shaped as well; the public consequences of a president's illness were all too apparent when Eisenhower suffered his first heart attack, in office, and the stock market experienced its greatest drop since the 1929 Depression.

Kennedy and Lincoln: A Striking Parallel

Many comparisons have been drawn between the

presidencies and fates of Abraham Lincoln and John F. Kennedy, but their mutual poor health has rarely been addressed. Lincoln and Kennedy both suffered from hereditary diseases that were considered incurable in their lifetimes. Lincoln was a victim of Marfan's Syndrome, an inherited dysfunction of the connective tissues of the body. Among other effects, it precipitates aortic aneurisms, a leading cause of heart attacks. The hoarseness Lincoln reportedly experienced just before his assassination may have been an indication that he was in the final stages of the disease.

John Kennedy, on the other hand, suffered from Addison's Disease, a usually fatal dysfunction of the adrenal cortex whose symptoms include a noticeable bronzing of the skin. White House press releases covered up this problem by reporting that Kennedy sat under a sun lamp every day to keep his California complexion.

The assassinations of Lincoln and Kennedy were terrible blows to the nation, but perhaps for the men themselves death by bullet was preferable to the slow degeneration that their illnesses held in store.

Cleveland, Wilson, FDR: Playing Down the Truth

When Grover Cleveland was president, his doctors discovered a tumor on the roof of his mouth. After lengthy consultation, it was decided that the tumor had to be removed. The problem, however, was how to perform the operation without the public or the press finding out. It was feared that if the president's health appeared to be in jeopardy, an already troubled economic situation might descend into a panic. Finally, in a carefully orchestrated move, Cleveland was whisked onto a ship, and there the operation was performed. Surgeons successfully removed the upper left section of his jaw and replaced it with a piece of vulcanized rubber, the first prosthesis of this kind. After a brief recovery publicized as a holiday, Cleveland returned to his presidential duties. His secret was so closely guarded that it was not made public until well after he left office.

Evidence suggests that Woodrow Wilson may have suffered a series of minor strokes as early as 1896. On September 25, 1919, he was stricken by the first of several devastating strokes that left him helpless and the country deeply apprehensive. No one seemed to know exactly who was handling the affairs of state in the final six months of Wilson's term. During those months, no cabinet meetings were called. Wilson was confined to his bedroom; his wife Edith permitted him only one visitor a day. When his signature was required, Edith carried the official documents in to him and returned with a barely legible scrawl. White House scuttlebutt had it that Edith Wilson was actually running the country, but neither she nor Woodrow cared to confirm this. The presidency and the nation held to a course of bare-minimal government until Wilson's term was up. When Warren Harding stepped into office, the United States and perhaps the Wilsons themselves breathed a sigh of relief.

Franklin Delano Roosevelt, like John Kennedy, was a president who kept his disabilities to himself. He contracted polio as a grown man, during the summer of 1921 when he was vacationing at his family retreat on Campobello Island. He had just ended a full day of sailing (with a short stop to help put out a forest fire) and a brief dip in the icy lake. When he returned home in the evening he was too tired to dress for dinner. Soon he was feeling chills and complained of aches and pains all over his body. The next morning his temperature was 102 degrees, and by the afternoon he could not move his legs.

At first the family physician told the Roosevelts that it was merely a cold. A second doctor diagnosed FDR's condition as a blood clot on the spinal cord. Finally an orthopedist who was vacationing nearby informed Roosevelt that he had polio.

Throughout his illness and afterward, FDR kept a positive, optimistic attitude. Undeterred by his paralysis, he captured the governorship of New York and then the presidency. The public never realized he was confined to a wheelchair, or that he had to be lifted out of bed and carried to the bathroom. He could stand only with heavy metal leg braces, leaning on the arm of a companion. Fearing that the public would lose confidence in him if it realized the extent of his disability, Roosevelt allowed himself to be photographed either sitting or standing, but never walking, sitting in a wheelchair, or being carried. He seldom mentioned his polio publicly. Once he let down his guard and said, "If you had spent two years in bed trying to wiggle your big toe, after that everything else would seem easy."

The Presidents and Drink

Our presidents have been a fairly abstemious lot; the only really heavy drinkers among them seem to have been James Monroe, Ulysses S. Grant, Chester Arthur and Franklin Pierce. Rutherford B. Hayes, James K. Polk and Abraham Lincoln never drank at all. Andrew Johnson was once wrongly accused of being a heavy drinker, when he became inebriated at his vice-presidential inauguration. Actually, he had had a sip of brandy before the inauguration, but because he never drank he could not handle it. Abe Lincoln jumped to his defense saying, "In all the years I have known Andy Johnson, I have never known him to drink."

Theodore Roosevelt actually filed suit in court against a newspaper that ran an item accusing him of being a drunkard. During the trial, Roosevelt took the stand to as-

sert: "I have never drunk whiskey or a highball in my life
...At public dinners I sometimes drink a glass of champagne, or perhaps two." Obviously the jury believed TR;
they awarded him a clean reputation and six cents
damages.

Being linked with alcohol did not seem to worry William Henry Harrison. During the election of 1840, Harrison
used the symbols of his frontier soldiers—a log cabin and a
jug of hard cider—as his campaign banner. The public took
these emblems as a sign of down-to-earth toughness, and
the former general won the election. The banner was somewhat misleading, as Harrison never lived in a log cabin and
probably drank hard cider little, if at all.

A taste for good food and especially for fine wines
may shed some light on a nagging complaint of Thomas Jefferson's. Our third president drank red wine with his meals
nearly all his life, and he suffered from severe migraine
headaches throughout adulthood and well into his retirement from public service. Studies now show that red wine
contains a large amount of tyramine, a chemical known to
induce headaches in many people.

Grant and the Battle of the Bottle

Ulysses S. Grant was one of a very few presidents
who did undergo some serious bouts with the bottle. During
the Civil War complaints of Grant's drinking problem
reached Abraham Lincoln. Lincoln, pleased with Grant's
performance, reportedly replied that whatever brand of
whiskey Grant was drinking, he wanted to order some for
the rest of his generals. This story was widely publicized,
but when reporters asked Abe himself whether he had
made that statement, the president said that he had not.

Throughout his life, Ulysses S. Grant had his ups and
downs, and when he had the downs he drank. All but one

time. Years after Grant left office he was stricken with cancer of the throat. Weakened, penniless, and dying, Grant faced the toughest battle of his life. He successfully replenished his family's finances by writing his best-selling memoirs. Although in constant pain, he worked for eight months, often through the night, to complete his project. He knew it was a race against death. At one point he wrote to his doctor, "I am thankful for the providential extension of my time to enable me to continue my work." The two-volume set assured his wife and family a comfortable income for the rest of their lives.

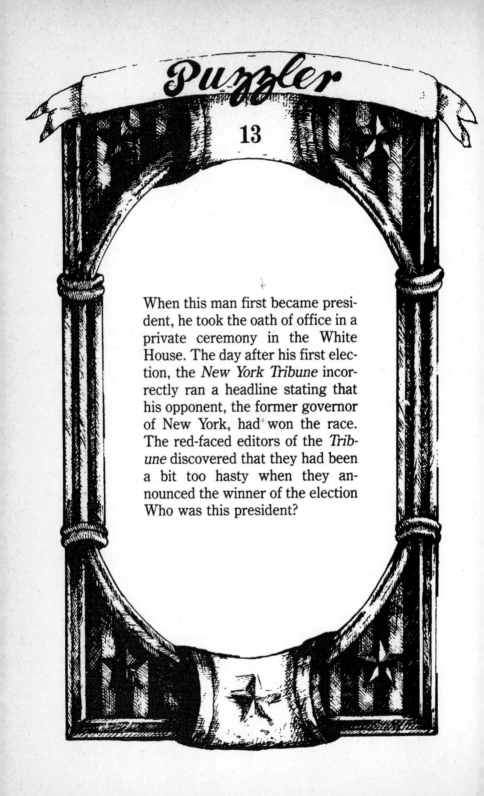

Puzzler

13

When this man first became president, he took the oath of office in a private ceremony in the White House. The day after his first election, the *New York Tribune* incorrectly ran a headline stating that his opponent, the former governor of New York, had won the race. The red-faced editors of the *Tribune* discovered that they had been a bit too hasty when they announced the winner of the election Who was this president?

13

Mistresses And Girlfriends

*Of course, I may go into a strange bedroom now
and then. That I don't want you to write about,
but otherwise you can write everything.*

—Lyndon B. Johnson

Almost as much can be said about the sex lives of
American presidents as about the power of the presidency itself. Certainly, the relationship between sex and
power is not coincidental, or alien, to political life in the
United States. It has always been a formidable political
weapon, as well as an interesting measure of the morals and
personalities of the men who were president.

During the 1800 presidential election, John Adams
was surprised to hear a rumor that he had just acquired two
new mistresses. Word had it that he had personally sent
General Thomas Pinckney, the brother of his running mate,
overseas to obtain four mistresses: two for Pinckney, and
two for Adams himself.

"I do declare if this be true," Adams protested, "General Pinckney has kept them all for himself and cheated me
out of my two."

Abigail Adams was less amused. "I have heard so
many lies and falsehoods propagated to answer electioneering purposes that I am disgusted with the world," she said.

Through the years of our country's history, candi-

119

dates for every office have been subjected to slander and attacks concerning alleged or real illicit affairs. The accusations have not always been generated by the press or the public; candidates often savage each other mercilessly. When Richard Nixon was running against Helen Gahagan Douglas for reelection to the United States Senate, he sought to discredit both his opponent and President Truman in one fell swoop. At a large campaign rally, Nixon answered a question that was no doubt planted by a campaign aide. "I'm not suggesting that any hanky-panky is going on between Harry Truman and my opponent," said Senator Nixon, "But lots of knowledgeable people claim where there is smoke there must be fire." Of course Bess Truman did not believe it for a minute. When she was asked by the women of her bridge club if she were worried about Harry running around loose in Washington among all of the pretty secretaries, Bess merely replied, "No."

Her trusting nature is in sharp contrast to Mary Todd Lincoln's suspicious mind. In response to an innocent comment about a business meeting the president had had with a lady in his office, Mrs. Lincoln burst out, "That's impossible; I never allow my husband alone with any woman."

Harry Truman once said that he had heard rumors when he entered the White House that President Chester Arthur had a mistress actually living there with him. James Buchanan was the subject of similar rumors. At the age of twenty-seven, young lawyer Buchanan had fallen in love with beautiful and wealthy Anne Coleman of Pennsylvania. The young couple was engaged, but their marriage plans were cut short when they had a lover's spat and she committed suicide. The grief-stricken Buchanan vowed never to marry. When he became America's only bachelor president thirty-seven years later, rumors circulated that he kept a mistress in the White House.

Even George Washington was not immune to gossip. One story told of his infatuation with the married daughter of an old friend. Her name was Sally Fairfax. Washington was not yet married to Martha, but surviving letters indicate that he continued to have feelings for Sally even after his marriage to Martha.

Grover Cleveland was accused of fathering a son with widow Maria Crofts Halpin, and he admitted he had. The information was released just before the presidential election and, since the story was true, Cleveland decided not to deny it. Instead, he admitted to the country that he was indeed a human being, that human beings do make mistakes, and that he had made one. James Blaine, Cleveland's opponent in the presidential race, had a personal life that seemed impeccable, but had a somewhat dubious political reputation. Cleveland had an excellent political reputation. Impressed with Cleveland's honesty, most of the major newspapers surprisingly endorsed Cleveland over Blaine, reasoning that a person should be placed in the position for which he was best suited. Blaine had a good reputation in his private life so he should remain a private citizen. Cleveland, on the other hand, had a good reputation as a public servant, so he should be placed in the office of the president.

Thomas Jefferson probably fathered more illegitimate children than any other president. When Jefferson's wife died, he had promised her on her deathbed that he would never remarry. He kept his promise, although he did not lead a life of celibacy. It was after a doomed love affair with Maria Cosway, the wife of a wealthy Englishman, that Jefferson settled into a long relationship with his slave Sally Hemings. Hemings was actually his wife's half-sister, the daughter of Jefferson's father-in-law and a slave named Betty Hemings. Sally Hemings eventually accompanied Jefferson to Europe when he was appointed minister to France, and it was there that the first of their five children was conceived.

Jimmy Carter created quite a stir when he admitted

121

in a *Playboy* magazine interview that he "lusted" in his heart. Senator Warren G. Harding lusted in more practical places; he reportedly had sexual relations with one of his mistresses in the closet of his Senate office. The young lady in question was Nan Britton, a pretty friend of the family— friend, that is, until she became pregnant by then President Warren G. Harding. Convinced that divorce was out of the question, Harding supported the lady and her illegitimate child, Elizabeth Ann. When Harding died in office, however, the payments stopped, so Nan Britton went to Dr. George Harding, father of the deceased president. She asked for only a portion of his son's estate so that she could afford to raise Harding's child. Dr. Harding flatly refused, so Nan proceeded to write a book entitled *The President's Daughter.* She overcame several attempts to stop publication, and her book was finally released. It became a bestseller and enabled Nan and her daughter to disappear into the sunset with enough money to live comfortably. Nan's footnote to history was an organization she formed called the Elizabeth Ann Guild for Unwed Mothers.

Even before Nan Britton came into Warren G. Harding's life, he had been seeing another lady, Carrie Phillips, the wife of a prominent merchant in Harding's home town of Marion, Ohio. When Mrs. Phillips put pressure on Warren to get a divorce, he severed the relationship. Warren's father was well aware of his son's meanderings. He told his son that if Warren were a girl, he would always "be in the family way because you can't say no."

"No" is just what General George C. Marshall said to Dwight D. Eisenhower when Ike asked to be relieved of duty so that he could get a divorce and marry Kay Summersby. Supposedly, Marshall had Eisenhower talk with General Omar Bradley, who prevented the future president from making what he called a serious mistake.

When Franklin D. Roosevelt's love letters from Lucy Mercer were discovered by Eleanor, Roosevelt found himself set upon by two angry women. On the one hand, Eleanor refused to live with him any longer if he continued seeing his mistress. On the other hand, his mother, Sara Roosevelt, forbade him to divorce Eleanor, warning that it would ruin his political career. Roosevelt acquiesced to the wishes of both women, but life was never really the same for the Roosevelts.

When Franklin made it to the White House, he found another lady to give his attentions to: Eleanor's own secretary, Missy LeHand. According to Roosevelt's son Elliott, Eleanor knew about the situation and actually allowed Franklin and Missy to have adjoining rooms when they were both staying at the White House. Missy suffered a stroke and died in 1941, and Franklin once again turned to Lucy Mercer as a lover. He kept their meetings secret from Eleanor but not from anyone else. When Franklin Roosevelt died of a cerebral hemorrhage, Eleanor discovered that Lucy had been at his side. She was furious when she discovered that her own daughter, Anna, had known for quite a while that her father had been seeing Lucy in the White House whenever Mrs. Roosevelt was out of town. She was even more furious on learning that Anna had actually helped her father arrange some of the rendezvous.

According to a recent publication, Lady Bird Johnson knew about Lyndon's affair with the wealthy and beautiful Alice Glass. Lady Bird had more than enough time to discover the affair because it had reportedly been going on since Lyndon first went to Washington in 1937 and continued throughout his life. LBJ was known to be a flirt, and although he was quick to discuss extramarital affairs with close friends, the Alice Glass affair must have been the real thing, since he never discussed it with anyone. LBJ's name was also linked with that of Doris Kearns, a young writer who once wrote a derogatory article entitled "How to Dump LBJ in 1968" for *The New Republic*. For some reason the article and its author intrigued the president. When Kearns and Johnson met, they discussed the article at great length, and she was eventually offered a post in the Johnson White House. Her reason for being in the White House was not described precisely, and Kearns herself said, "What I think he really wanted was just somebody to talk to." After Johnson left the office, she continued to work for him intermittently at the LBJ ranch in Texas, and became a biographer of his. They remained fast friends for the balance of Johnson's life.

Fast friends are exactly what President John F. Kennedy had. Of course, they had to be fast because aides would sneak young ladies into the White House for an evening of fun and merriment when wife Jackie was out of town. Once, however, Mrs. Kennedy returned to the White House earlier than expected, and quick-thinking aides had to break up the party in the White House pool.

Kennedy has been linked with numerous actresses, models, secretaries, stewardesses, and various other women. A reporter, commenting on his extramarital affairs, once said, "If every woman that said she went to bed with John Kennedy actually had, the Oval Office would have had to have a waiting room the size of the Astrodome."

This comment might be apropos for most of the stories about presidential love-making. But what of the stories that are true? What do they tell us about the character of the men who have occupied the office of the president?

Moral judgements aside, these stories time and time again reveal men who were romantics. Each showed it in a different way. Reportedly, George Washington would often fall madly in love, as did Thomas Jefferson and Warren Harding. Jefferson found it romantic to promise his dying wife that he would never remarry. James Buchanan similarly vowed that he could never love another. Harry Truman, in his own way, was a romantic; he chose to be faithful to one woman because being faithful is also romantic.

Dreamers tend to be romantics; without romance

they could not keep their dreams alive. President Woodrow Wilson once wrote, "I am absolutely dependent on intimate love for the right and free and most effective use of my powers." Many of these men would have agreed. They had to be in love, whether it was with a wife, a lover, or a memory.

"Miracle on 34th Street" Proof

There has been much debate in the last two hundred years about Sally Hemings's children; were they in fact fathered by Thomas Jefferson? Jefferson's own grandson said that Sally "had children which resembled Mr. Jefferson so closely that it was plain that they had his blood in their veins." On March 13, 1873, a man named Madison Hemings shocked the world when he wrote in the *Pike County Republican* that he was the son of Thomas Jefferson and Sally Hemings. He asserted that Jefferson fathered four other children by Sally Hemings. Tom, the oldest, supposedly died in infancy. Another son, Beverly, was born in 1798, and he left Monticello in 1822. He married a white woman in Maryland and lived the rest of his life as a white man. Another child, Harriet, also passed as white. She was born in 1801 and married a white man in Washington. The two raised a family and no one ever suspected her or her children's origins. Eston, another son, was born in 1808 and eventually moved to Wisconsin with his black wife. He died leaving three children. Madison Hemings stated that he himself was born in 1805 and married the granddaughter of a slave. He moved to Ohio where he worked as a carpenter. He died just four years after making his shocking statements.

Another Monticello slave wrote that, "Sally Hemings (mother to my old friend Madison Hemings), was employed as his (Jefferson's) chamber maid, and that Mr. Jefferson was on the most intimate terms with her; that, in fact, she was his concubine." Supposedly, Sally's children were given their freedom because of an agreement the president made with Sally while they were together in France. The only way Jefferson could convince her to return to the United States was to promise to guarantee her children's freedom.

Recently, when a descendant of Thomas Jefferson was asked if the story were valid, he replied, "Do you remember the movie 'Miracle on 34th Street'? In the movie certain people took a man claiming to be Santa Claus to court complaining he was a fraud. The movie ended when the judge decided that the man must be Santa Claus because the United States Post Office sent letters addressed to Santa Claus to the defendant. Well," he continued, "every year the United States government invites the descendants of Mr. Jefferson for a ceremony commemorating his birth, and every year the descendants of Sally Hemings are invited. That's 'The Miracle on 34th Street' proof. If the United States government believes it, it's good enough for me."

Did You Hear the One About...?

Woodrow Wilson was barely president a year when tragedy struck. After almost twenty years of marriage, his wife Ellen died at the age of fifty-four. The president was grief-stricken. It was almost a year later, when he met Edith Bolling Galt, the widow of Norman Galt, owner of an exclusive Washington jewelry store. Soon the president and Mrs. Galt were caught up in a whirlwind romance, much to the delight of some and the dismay of other Americans. Many people felt that it was just too soon after his wife's death. Others responded like school children excited that their teacher has a boyfriend. Just like school children, they were busy trading a host of Woodrow Wilson—Edith Galt jokes. To add to the merriment, a newspaper incorrectly published a story about the president and his lady. Instead of stating that the president "spent the rest of the evening entertaining Mrs. Galt in the White House," it was printed that he "spent the rest of the evening entering Mrs. Galt in the White House." Although the error was caught after the first edition, the damage was done, and the public got a good laugh, much to the embarrassment of the president and the future First Lady. Finally, after an exciting eight-month courtship, they were married on the eighteenth of December, 1915. People across America were asking each other, "What did Mrs. Galt do when the president asked her to marry him?" The answer: "She fell out of bed!"

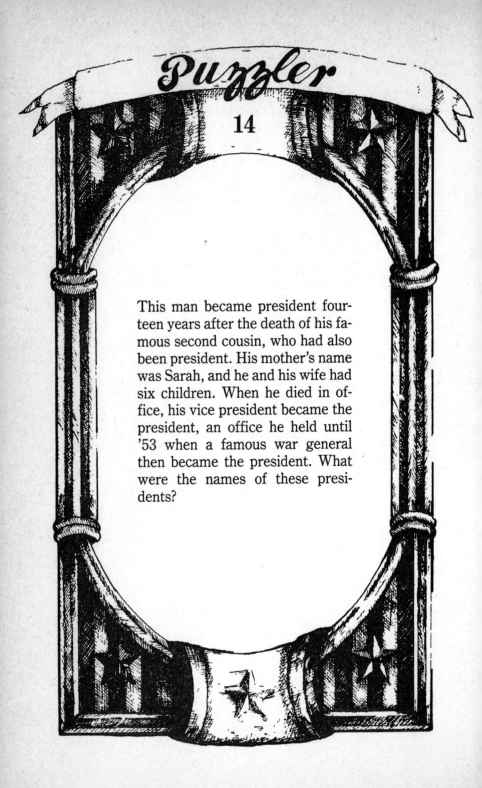

This man became president fourteen years after the death of his famous second cousin, who had also been president. His mother's name was Sarah, and he and his wife had six children. When he died in office, his vice president became the president, an office he held until '53 when a famous war general then became the president. What were the names of these presidents?

14

Relatives And Ancestors

I am not quite as interested in who my grand-father was as I am in what his grandson will become.

—*Abraham Lincoln*

Alexander Hamilton once referred to John Adams as "a self-made aristocrat." This comment was inspired, no doubt, by the fact that Adams was the son of a shoe-maker who had no apparent links with the ruling class of the day. Critics of Abraham Lincoln often spoke of his lack of background and breeding. In fact, despite their humble upbringings, both John Adams and Abraham Lincoln had kinships to famous contemporaries of the day and even to British royalty. The small size of the young nation and the limited number of different families in the upper strata of society make these relationships between ruling and work-ing classes seem less remarkable, almost inevitable.

But there were presidents—Andrew Jackson, James K. Polk, Millard Fillmore and Andrew Johnson—who had virtually no links to the ruling class or to British royalty. It appears that leaders of the United States can be selected from any part of our society. The aristocratic backgrounds of George Washington and Franklin Roosevelt are in stark contrast to the poor farmer backgrounds of Millard Fillmore and Andrew Johnson, who were both indentured servants at one point in their lives. Between those two extremes are the middle-America backgrounds of Harry Truman and Ronald Reagan. The majority of the presidents of the United States came from middle class backgrounds with the remainder divided between aristocrats and dirt-poor farmers.

On September 14, 1975, Pope Paul VI completed the final steps in canonizing Elizabeth Ann Bayley Seaton as Saint Elizabeth Ann Seaton, the first American-born Catholic saint. Mother Seaton was originally a Protestant, but she shocked and dismayed her family by converting to Catholicism after the death of her husband, William M. Seaton. She greatly influenced her nephew James Roosevelt Bayley. Bayley eventually followed his Aunt Betsey, once again shocking the family by converting to Catholicism. He had originally been an Episcopal priest but in 1841 became a priest in the Catholic Church of Rome. James's action outraged his father, who omitted James from any inheritance. In 1872 Father James Roosevelt Bayley became the eighth archbishop of Baltimore. For a time there was talk that he would eventually become a cardinal. Many people found it ironic that a Catholic cardinal would come from the center of America's Protestant establishment; the *New York Herald* called it "poetic fitness" that a Roosevelt might become the first American cardinal. The paper added that he had "the face of a bishop and a ruler."

That the Roosevelt family's first connection with Catholicism produced a saint and an archbishop is perhaps the best proof that when the Roosevelts did anything, they did it in a big way. Franklin Roosevelt once began a speech to the Daughters of the American Revolution, "Fellow immigrants." He pointed out in that same speech that not one of his ancestors arrived in this country after 1776. The Roosevelt clan, in fact, boasts quite a few ancestors who were passengers on the *Mayflower*. Even Teddy Roosevelt's presidential yacht was appropriately named *Mayflower*.

Another illustrious Roosevelt relative was Nicholas

Roosevelt, inventor of the steamboat. It is not well known that he had the original patent on the invention and took Robert J. Fulton to court for patent infringement. Roger Taney, who later became an outstanding chief justice of the Supreme Court, represented Roosevelt in the suit. It was Taney's opinion that Nicholas would have won the suit if he had possessed the funding to continue the proceedings. Nicholas Roosevelt was an Oyster Bay Roosevelt, as was Teddy Roosevelt; Franklin was from the Roosevelt clan usually referred to as the Hyde Park Roosevelts.

Teddy Roosevelt was also related to another president, and although they did not have a common surname they were technically closer on the family tree than were Teddy and Franklin. Through the Van Schaick family (Teddy's great-grandmother), Teddy was a third cousin twice removed to President Martin Van Buren.

Franklin also had a presidential relative besides Teddy. Through Franklin's mother's family, the Delanos, Franklin Roosevelt was a fourth cousin once removed to President Ulysses S. Grant. Once again, this relationship is closer than that of Teddy and Franklin.

In a more distant relationship, Ulysses S. Grant was sixth cousin once removed to President Grover Cleveland. Still further apart are Richard Nixon's relationships to two other United States presidents; Nixon is a seventh cousin twice removed to William Howard Taft, and an eighth cousin once removed to Herbert Hoover. Outside of the direct linear relationship of the two Adamses and the two Harrisons, the closest relationships between two presidents are those of Zachary Taylor and James Madison, who were second cousins, and James Madison and George Washington, who were first cousins twice removed.

Many cousins of presidents are distinguished figures in American history. It was at the Wigwam convention center in Chicago during the May 1860 Republican National Convention that convention delegate William Delano of Ohio, a cousin of Franklin D. Roosevelt, gave this short nominating speech: "I rise on behalf of a portion of the delegation from Ohio, to put in nomination the man who can split rails and maul Democrats—Abraham Lincoln." When Lincoln won that election, he appointed his cousin Salmon P. Chase secretary of the United States Treasury. Chase, who was Lincoln's fourth cousin once removed, experienced far greater success in his political career than did Lincoln himself, with one exception; he was relentless in his pursuit of, but he never attained, the presidency. During his long political career, he served as United States senator from Ohio, governor of Ohio, secretary of the Treasury, and chief justice of the Supreme Court. He unsuccessfully challenged Lincoln for the Republican nomination in 1864. Lincoln's success and Chase's failure to reach the presidency may be a reflection of their personalities, which were a study in contrasts. Chase lacked the sense of humor and quick wit of his cousin Abe. Where Lincoln appeared humble and kind, Chase was perceived as cold and overly ambitious.

Another study in contrasts might be found in President James A. Garfield and his fifth cousin once removed, Brigham Young. The flamboyant leader of the Mormon Church often boasted that he had only eleven days of formal education, while the learned Garfield was very proud of his classical education. Garfield was a devoted family man with seven children, but he was not nearly the family man that his cousin Brigham was. Young, by most accounts, fathered fifty-six children with some two dozen wives. Like his president-cousin, Brigham was also a politician, serving as the first governor of the Utah Territory. In addition to being Garfield's cousin once removed, he became a governor once removed when President James Buchanan sent in government troops and physically removed him from office. He continued as president of the Mormon Church for the remainder of his life and died in 1877, four years before his cousin James died from an assassin's bullet.

When Ulysses S. Grant was elected president, he appointed his cousin Richard Henry Dana to represent the United States as minister to England, although the Senate failed to confirm the appointment. Like his popular cousin Ulysses, Dana had aided the North during the War Between the States; as an attorney, he successfully convinced the United States Supreme Court to sustain the Northern blockade of Southern ports. Although Dana is best known as the author of *Two Years Before the Mast,* he was very active in political causes. In 1848 he helped found the anti-slavery Free Soil Party. Conversely, his cousin Ulysses was never thought of as an author, but the only financially successful effort of Grant's entire life was his best-selling memoirs, which he wrote shortly before his death.

When Thomas Jefferson became the third president of the United States, his cousin was already chief justice of the Supreme Court. Chief Justice John Marshall was second cousin once removed to President Jefferson. Marshall, in fact, administered the oath of office to Jefferson. Like his cousin, John Marshall was a dropout from the College of William and Mary in Virginia. Just as Jefferson served as secretary of state under George Washington, so Marshall served as secretary of state under John Adams. Marshall is credited with establishing the power of the Supreme Court when he declared a law that Congress passed to be unconstitutional. In doing so, he established the power of the Supreme Court to serve as a balance to the other two branches of government.

Although it is widely known that John Adams did much to serve his country, it is his cousin Samuel Adams who is credited with molding public opinion toward revolution and separation from England. Calvin Coolidge's second cousin six times removed was the famous Revolutionary War General Israel Putnam. Gerald Ford's five-great grandfather Ezra Chase was a Massachusetts Militia Minute Man during the Revolutionary War.

As is true for most of America's presidents, James Buchanan's roots go across the ocean to Great Britain. Buchanan's family, however, can be traced not only to an English heritage but to Sir Walter Buchanan and, from him, directly to Robert II, King of Scots. George Washington, John Quincy Adams and Abraham Lincoln can all be traced back to Edward I, King of England, while Presidents Jefferson, Monroe, Harrison, Grant, Garfield, Taft, and Nixon can claim ties to an assortment of European royalty. Of the two Roosevelts, only Teddy is a descendant of Robert III, King of Scots. Franklin D. Roosevelt makes up for his lack of royal connection through one of the most remarkable of relationships. The two giants of the Second World War, Winston Churchill and Franklin D. Roosevelt, were linked by more than just the burdens of war; the British prime minister who stirred his countrymen by telling them, "This was their finest hour," and the American president who told his people, "The only thing we have to fear is fear itself," were seventh cousins once removed, eighth cousins, and eighth cousins twice removed through three different lines of their families.

Many questions arise when contemplating the genealogy of the men who were our presidents and our leaders. Is there a genetic link to greatness or, with the right catalyst, will a seemingly common person have the capacity to become a great leader? Judging from the backgrounds of the thirty-nine presidents, both premises may be true. The spark of leadership seems to be stimulated by need; whenever this country was in dire need of true leadership, and nothing less than greatness would do, nature or luck or phenomenon somehow came through and provided us with the leadership we needed. It is tempting to consider that somewhere in the populace of this country exists another Abraham Lincoln or Franklin Roosevelt ready to emerge if the need arises.

Lincoln's Historic Ties

King Edward I of England reigned in the 1300s. He

was nicknamed "Longshanks" because of his long legs and towering hight. Exactly twenty-six generations later, a direct descendant of Edward I, Abraham Lincoln, became the sixteenth president of the United States. One of his nicknames was "Long 'un" because of his long legs and towering height. While ruling England, King Edward I perceived an injustice and took legal steps to correct it. He decreed that large land barons be required to prove ownership of newly acquired properties, thus freeing many peasants from the grip of unscrupulous landlords. Twenty-six generations later, Lincoln also saw an injustice in his country and took legal steps to correct it; one of his actions as president was to free the slaves.

During Edward I's reign, a man named Robert Bruce had himself crowned King of Scots in defiance of Edward's authority, an action which divided the country and caused a war that lasted many years. A little more than five hundred years later, Jefferson Davis was defiantly inaugurated president of the Confederate States of America. Lincoln's country was divided and at war.

The Booth Connection

In 1842, a young Richard Booth sailed for Baltimore, Maryland, where he planned to meet the father he had not seen in twenty-one years. When Richard was just an infant, his father, Junius Brutus Booth, had left his wife, Adelaide Delannoy Booth, and son in England, to further his already successful acting career in the United States. The elder Booth did so well in America that he had been able to send money to support his wife and son.

When Richard reached Baltimore, he met with his father and discovered that his father had not left England alone; Junius had taken a London flower girl with him, and by her he had fathered ten more children. Richard informed his mother, who eventually came to America and divorced

Junius. Although the young Booth had nothing further to do with his father, he still carried his father's name. The fact that two of his half-brothers went on to successful acting careers and toured throughout the United States was a constant reminder of his father's second family.

One of those half-brothers was a man who changed history: John Wilkes Booth, the man who assassinated Abraham Lincoln. The shame and disgust that Adelaide's son must have felt for his half-brother might have been alleviated had he known that his family's influence on American history was not all negative. On his mother's side was a cousin who would also affect the course of history, in a positive way: Franklin Delano Roosevelt.

The Ironic Victim

Richard M. Nixon won his first political campaign in 1946 by taking a hard line on communism. After his reelection to the House of Representatives in 1948, he was appointed to the House Committee on Un-American Activities. It was through his actions on this committee that Nixon first gained national prominence. He relentlessly pushed for the conviction of Alger Hiss, a former State Department aide accused of being a communist. In 1950, Nixon successfully ran for the United States Senate against Helen Gahagan Douglas. The emphasis of his campaign strategy was to link Douglas to various communist organizations. Even after Nixon left the United States Senate in order to become vice president, the communist hysteria continued in both houses of Congress.

In 1955, when Nixon was in the process of seeking a second term as vice president, a Senate report on Un-American Activities in California declared that communism was still rampant in Hollywood. In response to this charge, movie industry producers met in New York and issued the "Waldorf Declaration," which stated that none of them would ever knowingly employ communists or communist sympathizers. In effect, they agreed to blacklist anyone who appeared to be a communist. This declaration was extended to cover any person who had refused to answer any questions under oath before any Congressional Committee on Un-American Activities.

In 1956, a year after the Eisenhower-Nixon ticket was reelected, a movie entitled *Friendly Persuasion* was seen in local movie theatres. It became very popular; soon everyone was listening to Pat Boone sing the theme song, "Thee I Love." The Academy of Arts and Sciences nominated the movie for at least six major Academy Awards, including Best Picture, Best Director, Best Song and Best Screen Play. Michael Wilson, who had adapted the novel, *The Friendly Persuasion,* into a screenplay, however, was found to be ineligible for the award since he was on the Hollywood blacklist, and his name was removed from contention. The movie was condemned by association, and failed to win a single Academy Award.

The irony is that the novel, *The Friendly Persuasion,* was based upon the lives of Richard M. Nixon's Quaker great-grandparents. The author of *The Friendly Persuasion,* Jessamyn West, was Nixon's first cousin once removed. She wrote the story about her grandparents as told to her by her mother. West's mother and Richard Nixon's maternal grandfather were brother and sister; therefore, the subjects of the story were Nixon's great-grandparents. Had this relationship been publicized, would the weight of Nixon's anti-communist stance have cleared the movie of any suspicion? Or would Nixon's association with a communist movie have tainted his political career?

Tommy for President

Shortly after he was elected president, Woodrow Wilson made a brief stop in his home town. Arrangements were made for the president to visit the home of his aged aunt. When Wilson arrived at her house with a number of guests, she seemed a bit confused. Soon the conversation settled down to family matters, with Wilson's aunt asking him a number of questions. She would promptly put her ear trumpet to her ear after each question in order to receive the response. She asked him about his family, and he asked her about her health while reporters looked on intently. Wilson's aunt still called him Tommy, which was what everyone called him as a young boy.

Finally, the president's aunt proved to the world that she had not seen a paper in many years. She turned to Wilson and asked him what he was doing for a living now. The reporters suppressed giggles as they waited for Wilson to explain that he had just recently been elected president of the United States. The expression on his aunt's face turned into a frown when she heard his answer. She slapped her ear trumpet into her lap, refusing to hear any more folderol, and replied, "Don't be ridiculous!"

This president began his career as a Democrat. When he visited the children of a Head Start Program, they called him "Mr. Jellybean" because he would give each child a handful of jellybeans, the children little knowing that "Mr. Jellybean" was really the president of the United States. When he wasn't handing out jellybeans to kids or occupied with the duties of the presidency, you could find him at his ranch, horsebackriding, a sport he took great pleasure in. Who was this interesting president?

15

Foods

Good to the last drop!

—Theodore Roosevelt

T he culinary tastes of the presidents have been as diverse as the men themselves. There are, however, a few revealing taste preferences shared by many presidents. For example, several chief executives, including Teddy Roosevelt, George Washington and Thomas Jefferson, have loved sweet potatoes. This shared taste might be merely the result of regional preference or availability, but it might also point to a special nutritional craving. Many doctors and nutritionists believe that we seek out the very vitamins and minerals our bodies need. Sweet potatoes are high in vitamins A, C, and E.

Other presidents have favored foods high in zinc and vitamins B1 and B2. In fact, the vitamins and minerals in abundance in most of the presidents' favorite foods are those contained in today's "stress formulated" vitamin tablets. It is altogether possible that these men learned how to cope with stress not only psychologically, but also physiologically, through some quirky additions to their diets.

Beyond modern nutritional theory, however, the food preferences of the presidents provide entertaining capsule

141

characterizations. Epicures square off against meat-and-potatoes men. Favorite childhood dishes move onto the menus for state dinners. Oddball concoctions astonish aides and White House staff, and sometimes a president has changed the way America dines.

There are also picky eaters among the presidents, and some telling aversions to particular foods. For example, although General Ulysses S. Grant proved his bravery on the battlefield many times, it is a little known fact that he could not stand the sight of blood, either in battle or at the dinner table. Since he would become nauseated at the very mention of blood, he refused to eat red meat unless all the juices had been cooked out of it.

Grant was also unique in his choice of breakfasts. Almost every morning, whether he was on a battlefield or at home, he would feast on a concoction of sliced cucumbers in a vinegar sauce. President William McKinley was a mess sergeant in the army, so he brought hotcakes and johnny-cakes at breakfast with him into the White House. Woodrow Wilson habitually started his morning with a half grapefruit and two raw eggs. Franklin Roosevelt preferred his eggs scrambled, especially if he scrambled them himself. He took great delight in preparing scrambled eggs for guests too.

Hannah Nixon, mother of Richard Nixon, once said, "Richard was the best potato masher I have ever known." Nixon was a "meat and potatoes man"; in addition to mashed potatoes, his favorite food was meatloaf. President Eisenhower's favorite victuals make Nixon's meatloaf and mashed potatoes sound like a gourmet meal. The President and Mrs. Eisenhower used to settle down at the end of a long day to eat TV dinners on TV trays, while watching one of Ike's favorite TV shows, usually a western.

Zachary Taylor went on a peculiar eating binge one hot day after attending a ceremony to lay the cornerstone for the Washington Monument. President Taylor returned home and consumed large amounts of cherries and milk over the course of the rest of the day. When his family begged him to stop eating so much, he just ate more, until he became violently ill. Five days later, President Taylor was dead. Whether or not his strange eating habits had anything to do with his demise is uncertain.

Gerald Ford used to enjoy cottage cheese smothered in ketchup for breakfast. Although this dish did not seem to pose a danger to his life, those who watched him eat the unusual combination may have gotten queasy stomachs. John F. Kennedy once ate a whole pot of clam chowder at one sitting, and the cook was said to be amazed at his performance. Rutherford B. Hayes and Grover Cleveland preferred corned beef and cabbage with vegetables, while James Buchanan devoured massive amounts of mashed potatoes and sauerkraut.

As for desserts, Dwright D. Eisenhower's favorite was prune whip. Ronald Reagan, who awakened America to fine distinctions among jelly beans (small gourmet-flavored Jelly Bellies were the ones to look for), actually likes fudge brownies best for dessert. Lyndon B. Johnson reportedly snacked on Fiddle Faddle, a candy-coated popcorn, and looked forward to corn pudding for dessert. Abraham Lincoln is said to have had a special favorite that his family called "Election Cake," a raisin cake with cranberries. Mrs. Lincoln would bake this cake to serve at election parties, or, in Lincoln's case, at defeat parties, since he lost far more elections than he ever won.

At least one president lost his reelection bid because of his eating habits. In the election campaign of 1840, supporters of Martin Van Buren circulated a statement that opponent William Henry Harrison would rather have a jug of hard cider than live in the White House. They meant to show Harrison as a man of crude tastes. But the statement had the opposite effect. Harrison supporters turned the motto upside down and declared Van Buren too sophisticated to run a country of rough and tumble pioneers. Rumors flew that Van Buren ate such luxuries as strawberries, raspberries, celery and cauliflower. As if that were not enough, Van Buren was shown in drawings eating off silver plates and using gold spoons. Meanwhile, the Harrison camp cultivated a "he-man" image, and spread the rumor that their candidate ate raw beef without salt. The country obviously had more hicks than sophisticates, and William Henry Harrison won the election. One of Van Buren's favorite dishes, by the way, was Salade a la Volaille, an elaborate chicken salad with artichoke hearts.

Woodrow Wilson also loved chicken salad and ate it whenever he could. In fact, poultry lovers abounded among the presidents. Abe Lincoln raved about Mary Todd Lincoln's chicken fricassee. Andrew Jackson's tastes were simpler; he had a passion for turkey hash. Both John Quincy Adams and William Howard Taft liked chicken croquettes. James Monroe feasted on chicken gumbo whenever Mrs. Monroe would prepare it. Franklin D. Roosevelt loved the way the Warm Springs cook prepared chicken and looked forward to having it whenever he was there.

Roosevelt's homesickness for Warm Springs cooking was often triggered by his unhappiness with meals served in the White House. From time to time he actually attempted to remove Henrietta Nesbitt from her position as housekeeper in charge of all food preparation. At one point Roosevelt exclaimed, "My stomach positively rebels at the thought of eating any more of that woman's food." In 1937, when Ernest Hemingway was invited to dinner at the White House, he confirmed Roosevelt's discouraged view of Nesbitt's cooking. Hemingway reported that the food was "the worst I've ever eaten....We had rainwater soup followed by rubber squab, a nice wilted salad and a cake some admirer had sent in. An enthusiastic but unskilled admirer." Eventually, when Franklin Roosevelt's mother died in 1941, he arranged for the Hyde Park cook to set up shop in the

White House family kitchen on the third floor.

When the United States capital was in Philadelphia, President George Washington was unhappy with the food he was being served there. He had a black slave named Hercules who was his cook back at Mount Vernon, and he wanted to bring him to Philadelphia. But there was one problem: Pennsylvania law required slaves to be given their freedom after living in the state six months. George wanted Hercules to cook for him while he was president, but he did not want to give the man his freedom and possibly lose the services of a master chef. In order to avoid losing Hercules as a legal slave, Washington devised a scheme whereby Hercules would stay and cook for him in Philadelphia, but twice each year—on the days just before the end of the required six months—he would return to Mount Vernon. The six-month residency started from day one each time Hercules returned to Philadelphia, where he soon became quite a popular figure.

Everyone knew Hercules as a snappy dresser and a clever man, too clever to put up with the system that Washington had devised to deprive him of his freedom. And yet, just like clockwork, Hercules continued to return to Mount Vernon twice each year—that is until the very end of Washington's last term of office. At that time the president's by then famous master chef disappeared into the night. Much to Washington's dismay, Hercules was never heard from again.

John F. Kennedy and his wife were criticized for bringing a French chef into the White House, but they were not the first First Family to do so. Thomas Jefferson, James Madison, Martin Van Buren, and Chester Arthur all hired French-born chefs or managers. Ulysses S. Grant used the services of an Italian chef, while William Howard Taft and Woodrow Wilson ate foods prepared under the direction of a Swedish chef.

Perhaps no man has done so much to influence the

eating habits of the American people as President Thomas Jefferson. He made such foods as spaghetti, ice cream, baked Alaska, Irish potatoes, olive oil, and tomatoes commonplace in America. During his frequent travels throughout Europe, he searched out new and exotic delicacies. On a trip to Italy he risked a jail sentence when he successfully sneaked two bags of a rare hybrid rice out of the country. This rice was so new that the Italian government had banned its export.

Jefferson had a special fondness for vegetables and salads. Dinner guests at Monticello reported having salads with dozens of different varieties of lettuce combined with cucumbers, cress, endive, radishes, chicory, mustard greens, chives, cabbage, spinach, peppergrass, asparagus and tomatoes.

Jefferson was always searching for different types of cooking and salad oils. "The olive," Jefferson once said, "is a tree least known in America, and yet most worthy of being known." He also experimented with sesame seeds, an exotic commodity that slaves had brought with them from Africa. Jefferson soon learned that these seeds could be made into a pure and light oil. He also popularized sprinkling whole sesame seeds on bread and cakes.

At Monticello, Jefferson cultivated an elaborate fruit and vegetable garden. Among the many new and little known vegetables that Jefferson grew were broccoli, globe and Jerusalem artichokes, cauliflower, celery, eggplant, and scallions. His culinary influence was not limited to the United States. When Jefferson served as United States Minister to France, he delighted the guests at an elaborate dinner party by serving Indian corn on the cob. The corn had been grown in Jefferson's own Paris garden.

The preparation of foods was just as important to Jeffersson as the variety. He personally collected and copied recipes from all over Europe. Because he was fluent in French, Italian, Spanish, German and Greek, he had little trouble locating and translating the recipes he needed. While in the White House, Jefferson personally supervised the French chefs. Dinners at the Jefferson White House were exciting experiences that established the president as one of the greatest epicures and connoisseurs of his day. White House dinner guests were often amazed at the elaborate meals that Jefferson and his chefs prepared. On one occasion, dinner guests marveled at "ice cream in the form of small balls. . .enclosed in cases of warm delicious pastry." Others spoke of tasting a dish called macaroni for the first time, while still others were surprised by the taste and texture of a dessert called meringue.

Jefferson's stature as a recognized horticulturist and gourmet is something of a footnote in his career as a statesman, inventor, and scientist. But it provides an enjoyable picture of a man who was endlessly curious as well as diligently committed to setting an example of fine living and dining at the White House.

The Turkey Who Came to Dinner, and to Vote

Sometime in the fall of 1863, the White House received as a gift from a group of turkey farmers a large live turkey for the White House Christmas dinner. President Lincoln's son Tad soon grew to love the turkey and made a pet of him. Tad even gave the turkey a name, calling him not Tom but Jack.

Everything seemed to be going well until shortly before Christmas, when young Tad Lincoln overheard one of the White House cooks mention the ultimate fate of Jack the Turkey. In tears, Tad ran into his father's office to tell him what fate the White House staff had planned for his pet. After President Lincoln listened intently to his son's problem, he pulled a sheet of paper from his desk drawer and began to write. The President's son was delighted to find that his father had written out a presidential pardon for the bird. The pardon was the first of its kind. Tad and Jack continued to be fast friends. Eventually Jack became a familiar fixture on the White House lawn.

Several months later, a voting booth was set up on the White House grounds to enable soldiers stationed in the capital to vote. The president, his son Tad, and a reporter were watching the long lines of soldiers waiting to enter the booth when suddenly Jack the Turkey stormed into the voting area. Amused, Lincoln turned to his son and asked if the turkey had come to vote. Tad, exhibiting some of the Lincoln wit, replied, "No, he is not of age yet." This delighted his father, and Lincoln took great pleasure in repeating Tad's quip to friends and associates.

The Clevelands' Baby

Grover Cleveland was the only president in our history to serve two non-consecutive terms in office. Cleveland was both the twenty-second and the twenty-fourth president, with Benjamin Harrison serving one term (1889-1893) between Cleveland's two terms.

Both of Cleveland's terms in office were marked by domestic milestones that captured the attention of the American public. During his first term, Cleveland married Frances Folson amid the clamor of society columnists. Then, while out of office, the Cleveland's first child, Ruth, was born. When the Clevelands reentered the White House, the news media were enamored with two-year-old "Baby Ruth" Cleveland. Soon the whole nation was reading about the president's baby.

At the same time, a small candy company on Ashland

Avenue in Chicago began to produce a new candy bar, a caramel and nut mixture covered with chocolate. In a flash of inspiration its creators named it after Baby Ruth Cleveland. The candy bar was an immediate success, and Baby Ruth bars are still a staple at candy counters throughout America. Ruth Cleveland's chance at immortality, however, has been threatened by the passage of time. Americans today, if queried, assume that Baby Ruth bars must have been named after Babe Ruth.

Ad Man Roosevelt

In 1907 coffee merchant Joel Clark set up his concession booth on the grounds of the Hermitage, the historic home of President Andrew Jackson. The occasion was a fair celebrating the one hundred sixtieth anniversary of Andrew Jackson's birth. Clark knew that President Theodore Roosevelt was expected to arrive in a matter of hours, and he hoped to get a glimpse of the president. Understandably proud of a new blend of coffee he had just introduced, Clark even hoped the president might stop to taste a cup. He had confidently named the new blend after the most celebrated hotel in all the South, the Maxwell House. But the events of that day went beyond any of Joel Clark's expectations.

In due course, the president of the United States and his entourage arrived at Clark's booth and settled down at the cafe tables provided. Clark poured the president a cup of his special brew and grinned proudly as hundreds of onlookers watched the president sip the coffee. After the first few sips, Clark began to worry that the president might not have a favorable comment about the new blend. He began to grope for the right words to coax an endorsement out of the president. But before Clark could say anything, Roosevelt took his final gulp of the drink, turned to the crowd, and exclaimed that it was, "Good to the last drop!"

Little did Clark or the crowd know just how important that comment would become. Roosevelt's ebullient endorsement still rings out across America, emblazoned on cans of Maxwell House coffee.

After the turmoil of President Johnson's administration, this man was inaugurated president of the United States in '69. After his re-election for a second term, his private secretary, among others, was accused of dishonesty. His second term vice-president was the first vice-president ever to be sworn in with a name totally different from the name he was given at birth. This president visited China after retiring from office on March 4. Who was this president?

16

Honesty And Character

Mother, I want to be an old-fashioned lawyer, an honest lawyer who can't be bought by crooks.

—Richard Nixon, aged twelve

The concepts of honesty and honor change with the times. It was not considered dishonest, for instance, for a government official in the early 1700s to give government printing jobs to his friends or family. Soldiers in the 1700s who sneaked around behind trees were not considered to be fighting fairly. How then do we pass judgement on the "honesty" of our presidents?

Many presidential biographers dodge this delicate question by ignoring awkward facts. For example, much has been made of the fact that George Washington refused to accept a salary while he served as commander-in-chief of the Continental Armies. He was entitled to payments of five hundred dollars per month as approved by the Continental Congress. Since he served in that capacity for almost eight years, he turned down a total of $48,000 in salary. But there is more to the story: although the general did turn down the salary, he instead requested and received an expense account. From 1775 to 1783, George Washington used this expense account to purchase an imported carriage, exotic wines, and expensive saddles. At the end of eight years, the

153

total amount charged on this expense account came to an astonishing $447,000, a far cry from the $48,000 he would have received in salary.

There is, however, even more to this story. Washington apparently expended much of his personal wealth in support of the war. How much is open to debate, but when the war began he was a very wealthy man, yet after the war he had to borrow the money to get to his own inauguration.

Thomas Jefferson also understood the advantage of an expense account. At a time when it cost less than two dollars to feed a family of four for a week, he ran up an eleven-thousand-dollar White House wine bill. In relation to the prices today, the figure would be equivalent to the total amount spent on wine by the last three presidential administrations.

Apparently, even "Honest Abe" padded his expense account. When Lincoln was serving in the United States House of Representatives, Congress allowed representatives eight dollars for every twenty miles traveled to the capital and back home. Horace Greeley wrote an expose in the *New York Tribune* pointing out that Congressman Lincoln had received a total mileage allowance of $2,601 for his two allowable round trips between Illinois and Washington, which works out to a distance of over 1600 miles for a single one-way trip, or about 700 miles farther than the actual distance.

After the article appeared, the Congressional Committee on Mileage "whitewashed" the issue; it concluded that it could find no one congressman guilty of fraud or wrongdoing because it had been up to the Committee itself to regulate and approve the mileage claims submitted. Because final responsibility to recognize errors in mileage rested upon the committee, not on the congressmen themselves, the committee had been at fault, not the congressmen. Lincoln's defense or rationalization might also have referred to the fact that the salary congressmen made in his day was barely subsistence, and that most other congressmen exaggerated their travel expenses. Not only was the whole issue forgotten, but surprisingly, it was never resurrected during Lincoln's campaign for the presidency.

Some questions of presidential honesty take a long time to surface. In the late evening of February 15, 1898, the United States battleship *Maine* pulled into the Havana harbor, suddenly blew up, and sank. Two hundred fifty-eight American lives were lost. Soon, throughout America, rang the battle cry, "Remember the *Maine!*" With the help of the Hearst newspapers, the American people were demanding war with Spain, and President William McKinley complied. Although the Spanish government insisted that the sinking was caused by an internal explosion, the United States government claimed that it was a deliberate Spanish attack. By April 24, the United States had won the war, thereby releasing Cuba from Spanish rule.

The extraordinary ending to this story came in 1976 when Admiral H.R. Rickover reopened an investigation into the true cause of the explosion and sinking of the *Maine.* The results were shocking; the inquiry showed that the explosion onboard the ship was accidental, most likely from one of the ship's stoves. Further, the report suggested that President McKinley himself had been aware that the sinking was an accident, but had declared war on Spain anyway.

Another untruth that came out of the Spanish-American War involved Teddy Roosevelt. It was true that he formed the Rough Riders, and it was true that he and his men charged up a hill. What was not correct was the name of the hill. Theodore Roosevelt and his band of Rough Riders actually charged up Kettle Hill, not San Juan Hill as Roosevelt claimed. The more exotic name made for better press, and most assuredly helped his presidential campaign two years later.

Is it dishonorable for a president to secretly record

conversations? Recent evidence suggests that several former presidents, in addition to Nixon, did just that in the Oval Office. The list of conversation-recorders includes Franklin D. Roosevelt, Dwight D. Eisenhower, and John F. Kennedy.

Presidents of the United States have, for the most part, been honest and sincere; their desire to do good for the country has been first in their minds. The aura of the presidency has an effect on all who take the office, and even the few presidents who had less than honest reputations felt an obligation once they entered the office to do right. Richard Nixon had the sincere desire to be a president who did great things, but somehow lost sight of that goal, and people recognized it. This, most of all, was his downfall. Nixon was once quoted as saying, "Sincerity is the thing that comes through on television." More typical of what we expect from our presidents is Grover Cleveland's statement: "I tried so hard to do right."

Johnson Does Unto Others

When Congressman Lyndon Baines Johnson first attempted to win a Senate seat in 1940, he lost the election by only 1,311 votes. Eight years later he came back and won the seat of Democratic senator from Texas by a very slim margin: only eighty-seven votes out of 900,000. The narrow victory won him the nickname "Landslide Lyndon."

Naturally, after such a close race there were cries that the election had been rigged. Years later, in 1977, Luis Salas came forward and confirmed those suspicions; he stated that, as an election judge, he knew that Johnson had approached Texas political boss George Parr and asked that he steal two hundred votes to ensure a Johnson victory. Parr had agreed, and the order went out to provide Johnson with enough votes to win. Former F.B.I. Agent Kellis Dibrell confirmed Salas's story. He stated that he had personally seen many voters' signatures on the polling lists in alphabetical order, in the same color ink, in the same handwriting.

Johnson himself joked about the allegations; he told a story of a little boy, walking down the street crying. When someone asked him why he was crying, he answered, "My father has been dead for two years, and yesterday he came into town to vote for Lydon Johnson, and he didn't even stop to say hello to his son."

Johnson biographer Doris Kearns Goodwin has suggested that Lyndon was a victim in 1940 of the same type of vote fraud of which he was accused in 1948. In 1940, Johnson originally had been declared the winner by more than five thousand votes, but one day later his opponent was declared the winner by 1,311 votes. The Texas Election Commission cited a rush of late returns as the reason for the contradictory information. It may be that, in 1948, Johnson had learned to fight fire with fire.

Practice Makes Perfect?

On the basis of his outstanding college career, Richard Nixon was granted an academic scholarship to Duke Law School in 1934. At Whittier College he had been a football player, an actor, president of the student body, and ranked second in the graduating class. In law school he continued to excel academically, standing third in his class. Law school classmates described Nixon as intense and serious about his studies; in fact, he was afraid that he was in over his head, and worried constantly about his grades. He felt that his entire future depended on his maintaining his academic standing.

In 1936, during his second year of law school, Nixon began to fear the possibility of losing his scholarship. One professor failed to release the class grades and standings on time, which only served to increase Nixon's anxiety. When he could no longer stand the suspense, he and two of his classmates, William Perdue and Fredrick Albrink, conspired to break into the professor's office and learn their grades. Since Nixon was the thinnest of the three, he was the one to slide through the transom over the professor's office door. Once inside, he let the other two students in, and they managed to find the keys to the professor's desk and read their grades. They left the professor's office without being noticed by any Duke Law School authorities.

Nixons' indirect involvement twenty-six years later in the Watergate break-in in Washington proved far more costly to him than the college prank at Duke. The 1972 arrests of seven men for breaking into Democratic National Convention headquarters at the Watergate Hotel precipitated Nixon's resignation from the presidency of the United States, the first such resignation ever.

Would Nixon have learned his lesson for good if he had been caught and reprimanded for his law school caper? It is possible that if he had been caught, he might have been expelled, and not just reprimanded, and then there might not have been a lawyer Nixon, a Congressman Nixon, etc. Perhaps his reprieve was only temporary; it took twenty-six years for his punishment to catch up to him.

This man served as both governor and senator of his state, and at the age of fifty he became vice president of the United States. After the death of the president, he succeeded to the office of chief executive of the land. He became the first United States president to be the subject of a serious impeachment vote in Congress. Although he retained his position, he failed to receive the nomination for reelection and thus was never elected in his own right. He left the White House and continued to be politically active. He died shorty after being elected to represent his state in Congress. Who was this Southern president?

Answers to the PQ Quiz

To compute your score: *All first choice answers given in the explanations automatically receive five points.* The number of points for the other possible answers is given in each explanation. Since there are forty questions worth five points, plus five bonus points, the highest possible score is 205. Because no president would have received a perfect score, the hypothetical scores of past presidents appear on the chart at the end of the explanations.

Question 1:
B—Most presidents' fathers fall into this category with the remainder falling into the older categories. Many presidents had fathers who were over forty-five when the president-to-be was born, so if you answered D give yourself four points, and two points for C. Since only three presidents' fathers fall into the twenty-four and younger category, give yourself one point for answer A.

Question 2:
B—Once again, the majority of presidents' mothers fall into this category. The next largest amount were in the younger category. You therefore get four points for answer A, one point for C and no points for D.

161

Question 3:
D—Eleven presidents were born in either October or November, more than in any other months. Answer A gets four points, C gets three points, and B gets two points. No presidents were born in the entire month of June and only one president was born in September.

Question 4:
A—This is a perfect example of a strong mother-influence. C is worth four points, B is worth two and D one.

Question 5:
C—More presidents were middle children than any other birth order position; George Washington, Theodore Roosevelt and Richard Nixon were all middle children, for instance. Give yourself four points for answer A and three points for answer B. If you answered D, you don't get any points because no president has been an only child. Franklin Roosevelt was the closest to being an only child since his older brother was twenty-eight years older, making Franklin closer in age to his brother's son than to his brother.

Question 6:
D—Most presidents were born in rural areas. Only two presidents were born in large cities: Theodore Roosevelt, who was born in New York City, and William Howard Taft, who was born in Cincinnati. Give yourself four points for answer C and three points for answer B. Sorry, only one point for answer A.

Question 7:
D—Almost two-thirds of the presidents' fathers were self-employed. Most were farmers, which is a type of laborer,

but they worked for themselves, not for someone else. Only one father, George Harding, was a doctor, and surprisingly there were only a few lawyers. Many presidents' fathers owned their own businesses. Answer A deserves three points, with B and C getting two points each.

Question 8:
B—Different was better to most of these men, so give your-self five points. Four points go to answer A and three points to answer D. There were some presidents who did not like their names, but they usually did something about it, like Thomas Woodrow Wilson and Stephen Grover Cleveland. Give yourself *two bonus points* if you did not like your name and did something about it. As far as answer C is concerned, do you really think these men wanted to blend in? No points for answer C.

Question 9:
D—This is a tricky question, because even if their childhoods were bad you would not hear much complaining from these men. The comment by Abraham Lincoln, "A person is as happy as he sets his mind to be," was echoed by many presidents before and after him. Give yourself three points for C, two points for B, and no points for answer A.

Question 10:
B—Some people might think of these women as a little too strong-willed, but they had great influence on their children. Sara Roosevelt and Rose Kennedy are two contemporary examples of such strong influence. Answer A gets four points. D should get two points, since only three presidents were less than ten years old when their mothers died. C is worth one point, but don't feel bad if C fits you because even kind historians would label Washington's and Jefferson's mothers as pains in the neck.

Question 11:
B—Many presidents were "mama's boys," including the obvious Franklin Roosevelt and the not-so-obvious Benjamin Harrison and James K. Polk. C gets four points, D two points, and A one point. Once again, George Washington and Thomas Jefferson fall into the one-point category.

Question 12:
B—Richard Nixon's and Ronald Reagan's fathers are perfect examples of answer B. A gets four points because it is close to B without the negative aspects of the personality. C gets three points, and D only one point, since only two presidents were born posthumously and only three were less than ten years old when their fathers died.

Question 13:
D—Because of very sickly childhoods, many presidents were confined to their homes for extended periods of time. Instead of hurting their academic abilities, confinement enhanced them because in most cases they became avid readers. C gets four points, B gets two points, and A only one point.

Question 14:
A—Advantage is often not all that much of an advantage in molding a Presidential Personality. Many of these men made whatever advantages they had themselves. B gets four points, C two points, and D no points. Give yourself *three bonus points* if you answered D for Question 9 and A for this question.

Question 15:
A—Once again, advantage does not win out, but attitude does; families of presidents did not discourage intellectual

achievement. B should get two points since few presidents' families have been able to pay for education. D gets one point, and C gets zero points.

Question 16:
A—The Oval Office has seen a long line of charmers. How else could they have mustered so many votes? Even before women could vote, charming the opposite sex was a political advantage. One of the reasons Abe Lincoln grew his beard was that a little girl told him that it would make him look handsome and ladies would tease their husbands into voting for him. C is worth four points, since it shows an interest in the opposite sex and in other people. B is worth two points; D is not worth any points, since it is unlikely a person running for office would ever try to avoid anyone who might have a vote.

Question 17:
D—Romantics in the White House were as abundant as charmers, and some, like George Washington, fell in love often. C is worth four points, B gets two, and A is another zero.

Question 18:
D—Presidents often turned to their spouses for advice and feedback on everything from politics to affairs of state. Four points for answer B, and C gets three points. No points for A since the presidents' mothers filled that position.

Question 19:
A—Thomas Jefferson's personality bursts out of Monticello, and one look at Harry Truman's house will substantiate answer A even more. B is worth three points, because

impressive personalities sometimes have impressive homes. C will get two points, with D commanding an impressive zero.

Question 20:
D—Teddy Roosevelt, Calvin Coolidge, John Kennedy, and many others were great animal lovers. C will give you three points, and B is worth two points; Harry Truman's daughter once said her Dad could take pets or leave them. A is a big zero.

Question 21:
B—Most presidents had strong like and dislikes when it came to food. Some were fanatics about what went into their stomachs. A is worth three points, and C is worth two points. Do not bother writing anything down for answer D; it has no points.

Question 22:
D—These hams would get in front of a flock of geese if the geese had voting rights. They were also long-winded. A visitor leaving Teddy Roosevelt's office after one lengthy meeting, when asked what he had said to the president, replied, "My name—after that he did all the talking." Give yourself four points for C, one point for B, and no points for A. However, Thomas Jefferson was a poor speaker, and always sent a written State of the Union message to Congress.

Question 23:
A—Minglers make good vote-getters, and getting votes is the name of the game. Obviously, answer B deserves at least four points, with C squeaking by with two points. D gets no points.

Question 24:
B—A long line of avid readers have occupied the White House, so bringing something to read is only natural. Answer A is worth three points because most presidential types would joke with the waiter. D gets two points, and C gets none.

Question 25:
D—Talk, talk, talk. How many politicians do not like to talk? Still, a lady at a dinner party once told Calvin Coolidge that she had made a bet with a friend that she could get Silent Cal to say more than two words. His reply: "You lose." Give yourself four points for answer C and two for answer B. No points for answer A.

Question 26:
C—Not only were many presidents avid readers, they were history buffs as well. The seasick pills were thrown in because until Kennedy no president had been in the Navy. After Kennedy, however, came four more Navy men. A would give you four points, B three points, and D one point.

Question 27:
C—Most of the effective presidents were good delegaters. There were not many presidential loners, but give yourself four points for answer D anyway for resourcefulness. Only two points for answer A, and no points for answer B.

Question 28:
D—Most people who have attained the presidency have been aggressive, although some have accepted the job reluctantly. Give yourself four points for answer C. The noble answer B is worth one point, and A is worth no points.

Question 29:
C—Reading is the favorite presidential pasttime, with outdoor activities coming in a close second, so give yourself four points for D. A is worth three points and B is worth zero.

Question 30:
B—Most presidents were persistent but not stupid. A is worth four points since some were persistent and not very good businessmen. D is worth two points, and C is worthless.

Question 31:
D—Historically, the presidents did not avoid problems or opportunities; they took charge. Answer C is worth four points, B is worth three, and A is worth zero.

Question 32:
D—Eventually they did succeed. Answer B is worth four points, C is worth two points, and A is worth nothing.

Question 33:
D—Not only would you find presidential types working late, but you would find their helpers working right along with them. People like Abraham Lincoln and Lyndon Johnson expected their aides to keep similar hours, sometimes well into the night. C gets you four points, and B gets you two, but do not give yourself any points for A.

Question 34:
B—Most of the presidents did not think about retirement until they got into the White House, and then they could not

wait to get out of the place. Give yourself four points for answer A and two points for answer D. No points go to the people who answered C.

Question 35:
A—Under Ronald Reagan's picture in his high school yearbook runs a slogan than many presidents would have agreed with: "Life is just one grand sweet song, so start the music." B is worth four points, C is worth one point, and D is worth nothing.

Question 36:
B—Most presidents were just average students. Only three were Phi Beta Kappas: John Quincy Adams, Chester Arthur and Theodore Roosevelt. William Howard Taft was second in his class at Yale while Ulysses S. Grant was at the very bottom of his class at West Point. These two men were exceptions rather than the rule. Give yourself three points for answering C, two points for A and only one point for D.

Question 37:
C—Lyndon Johnson was president of his class, but he only took the job because no one else wanted it. John Kennedy was voted "most likely to succeed," but the majority of presidents would probably fall under the category of "most friendly." Give yourself three points for B, one point for A and no points for D.

Question 38:
A and B—Most presidents entered the working world at a very young age. Jimmy Carter hawked roasted peanuts at the age of nine. Answer C deserves three points, and D gets one point.

Question 39:
D—Lyndon Johnson and Richard Nixon, like many other presidents, are perfect examples of believers in "love at first sight." Both of them proposed marriage to their future wives after only two dates. Harry Truman, on the other hand, knew his wife for twenty years before they married, but he once remarked that he had always had an affection for Bess. Give yourself two points for C, one for A, and none for B.

Question 40:
C—The majority of these men were early risers. A tremendous amount of energy allowed them little sleep. Jimmy Carter once said, "I can get up at nine and be rested or I can get up at six and be president." Answer A is worth four points, D is worth three, and B is worth zero. However, late riser Martin Van Buren was one of the exceptions, often sleeping well into the morning.

Presidential Quotient Chart

    To obtain your Presidential Quotient you must divide the total possible number of points (205) by your score on the Presidential Quotient Quiz. The closer your answer is to 1.0, the closer you are to being a perfect candidate for president of the United States. Only one president scored within the top range, and *no* president scored any worse a quotient than 2.97 (a mediocre chance at becoming president.)

Score Range	Quotient Range	Presidents
1 - 34	205 - 6.03	---
35 - 68	5.85 - 3.01	---
69 - 102	2.97 - 2.0	James Buchanan Franklin Pierce Warren G. Harding
103 - 137	1.99 -1.5	John Adams William McKinley Dwight D. Eisenhower Lyndon B. Johnson John F. Kennedy
138 - 171	1.49 - 1.2	Franklin D. Roosevelt Woodrow Wilson Harry S Truman Andrew Jackson James K. Polk
172 - 205	1.19 -1.0	Abraham Lincoln

Puzzler Answers

#1 — Although most of the clues point to Herbert Hoover as the correct answer, one does not: Herbert Hoover lived for thirty-one years after leaving the White House. He died of natural causes in 1967. The correct answer is Martin Van Buren, who died in 1862. While president, Van Buren was blamed for the panic of the 1830's.

#2 — If your answer to this question was Jimmy Carter, you were close but not correct. It was Harry Truman's father, John Anderson Truman, who was nicknamed "Peanuts," and Truman's brother, Vivian, helped out on the farm with Harry. Harry's blue uniform was the uniform of the Missouri National Guard.

#3 — The correct answer to this question was not John F. Kennedy, but Ronald Reagan. Although most facts were true for John F. Kennedy, one was not. Kennedy was not the first man to become president at his young age; Theodore Roosevelt succeeded to the presidency at the age of forty-two. Kennedy was forty-two when he was *elected*, but was actually forty-three by the time he was inaugurated. Ronald Reagan, the oldest president, is the correct answer for all the facts in this puzzler.

#4 — If your answer was Andrew Jackson, you were incorrect for more than one reason. Andrew Jackson purchased his estate, The Hermitage, a year *after* his marriage. Although his wife died before he entered the White House, she had lived to see him elected. Thomas Jefferson was the correct answer; he had originally named his estate The Hermitage, in reference to his bachelorhood. After his marriage, he renamed it Monticello. He returned to it after retiring from the presidency.

#5 — If your answer was Thomas Jefferson, try again. Jefferson was a *two*-term governor of Virginia. Woodrow Wilson was the one-term governor who went on to serve two terms as president. Born Thomas Woodrow Wilson, Wilson later dropped his first name in favor of his middle name.

#6 — Because the man who was shot was a *former* president at the time, Ronald Reagan is not the correct answer. It was Former President Theodore Roosevelt who was shot while leaving his Milwaukee hotel during his bid for an unprecedented non-consecutive third term.

#7 — Although most of the clues seem to point to John F. Kennedy, the correct answer to this puzzler was John Quincy Adams. Kennedy's congressional career was interrupted after only six years when he was elected to the Senate. It was John Quincy Adams who served seventeen years as a congressman, *after* his term as president.

#8 — If you thought it was Richard Nixon's dog Checkers who saved a presidential election, try again. Checkers' name was used to help Nixon in his vice-presidential bid. It was King Tut that saved a presidential election when it seemed that nothing would pick up the popularity of Candidate Herbert Hoover. A photo of Hoover with his dog, King Tut, helped humanize Hoover's image and win the election.

#9 — If you answered Harry Truman, you were close but not correct. Although most of the clues were true for Truman, one was not: Harry S. Truman *did* attend law school. He went to Kansas City School of Law from 1923 to 1925. The correct answer is Abraham Lincoln. Like Truman who fired General Douglas MacArthur, Lincoln fired the popular General George B. McClellan.

#10 — If you answered Ronald and Nancy Reagan, you were not correct; Nancy Davis never appeared in any of these films, and she did not meet her husband while performing in *The Black Tower*. The woman who met her husband while appearing in a community production of that play was Thelma "Pat" Ryan. She met and married Richard Nixon, an amateur actor in the production.

#11 — If you were sure that the answer to this puzzler was Harry Truman, you were close but not correct. It was Margaret Wilson, not Margaret Truman, who entertained the troops. Her father, Woodrow Wilson, was the man who narrowly defeated opponent Charles Evans Hughes.

#12 — Although most of the clues were true for John F. Kennedy, he did *not* sign an act prohibiting the killing of seals. The act was signed in 1897 by William McKinley, the twenty-fifth president of the United States, and the correct answer.

#13 — If your answer to this puzzler was Harry S Truman, you were close but not correct. Although most of the facts were true for Truman one was not: it was the *Chicago Tribune,* not the *New York Tribune,* that incorrectly called the results of the Truman-Dewey race. The *New York Tribune* incorrectly named Samuel Tilden the winner in the Hayes-Tilden race of 1876. The correct answer is Rutherford B. Hayes.

#14 — If you thought that the presidents involved were Roosevelt, Truman, and Eisenhower, you were close but not correct. Teddy and Franklin Roosevelt were not second cousins, but fifth cousins. Zachary Taylor was president fourteen years after the death of his second cousin James Madison, and the two presidents following Taylor were Millard Fillmore and former General Franklin Pierce.

#15 — Although Ronald Reagan recieved much publicity for his lavish gifts of jellybeans, it was another president who visited the Head Start Program, a program he created during his administration. Lyndon Johnson, thirty-sixth president, first thought of the jellybean gifts.

#16 — If Richard Nixon was your answer, you were close but not correct. Although most of the facts were true for Nixon, one was not: Richard Nixon left office August 9, 1974. Ulysses S. Grant left office March 4, 1877, after a presidency tainted by corruption. Like Nixon's vice president Gerald Ford, Grant's vice president Henry Rice Wilson had been born with a different name: Jeremiah Jones Colbaith.

#17 — If your answer to this puzzler was Andrew Johnson, you were close but not correct. Although Andrew Johnson was the subject of impeachment proceedings, he was not the first to be so. John Tyler is the correct answer. After he left the presidency he was elected to represent the state of Virginia in the *Confederate* Congress.

Back Cover Puzzler —

If your answer to this question was John F. Kennedy, you were close but not correct. Although most of the facts were true for Kennedy, one was not: Kennedy's assassin was never convicted. The correct answer was James A Garfield, twentieth president of the United States.

SOURCES

General

A Compilation of the Messages and Papers of the Presidents,
Vols. I–VII. Edited by the Joint Committee on Printing of
the House and Senate. Bureau of National Literature,
1897.

A Compilation of the Messages and Papers of the Presidents,
Vols. VIII–X. Edited by the Joint Committee on Printing of
the House and Senate. Bureau of National Literature, n.d.

Barclay, Barbara, *Our Presidents,* Promontory Press, 1976.

Bassett, Margaret. *Profiles and Portraits of American Presidents,*
new and updated edition. New York: David McKay Co.,
1976.

Bolton, Sarah K. *Lives of Poor Boys who Became Famous.* New
York: Thomas Y. Crowell Co., 1947.

Davis, Burke. *The Civil War: Strange & Fascinating Facts.* New
York: Fairfax Press, 1982.

Durant, John and Alice. *Pictorial History of American Presidents.*
New York: Castle Books, 1955.

Durant, John and Alice. *The Presidents of the United States,*
Vols. I and II. Miami, Fla.: A. A. Gaché & Son, 1981.

Encyclopedia of American Biography. Edited by Garraty, John A.,
Assoc. Ed. Sternstein, Jerome L. New York: Harper &
Row, 1974.

Felton, Bruce, and Fowler, Mark. *Felton & Fowler's Famous
Americans You Never Knew Existed.* New York: Stein and
Day, 1979.

Fisher, James Knox. *Our Presidents: Their Lives and History.*
Chicago: M. A. Donohue & Co., 1910.

Forney, John W. *Anecdotes of Public Men.* New York: Harber &
Brothers, 1973.

THE PRESIDENTIAL QUOTIENT

Frank, Sid, and Melick, Arden Davis. *The Presidents: Tidbits & Trivia*. Maplewood, N.J.: Hammond, Inc. 1982.

Freidel, Frank. *Our Country's Presidents*. Washington, D.C.: National Geographic Society, 1966.

Freidel, Frank. *The Presidents of the United States of America*. Washington, D.C.: White House Historical Assoc. and National Geographic Society, 1975.

Goodrich, Rev. C.A. *History of the United States of America, Third Edition*. Hartford, Conn.: 1823.

Hatch, Louis Clinton. *A History of the Vice-Presidency of the United States*. New York: The American Historical Society, 1934.

Kane, Joseph Nathan. *Facts About the Presidents: A Compilation of Biographical and Historical Date*. New York, Ace Books, 1976.

Lorant, Stefan. *The Glorious Burden: The History of the Presidency and Presidential Elections from George Washington to James Earl Carter, Jr.* Lenox, Mass.: Authors Edition, Inc., 1976.

May, John, with Marten, Michael; Brittain, David; Chesterman, John; and Torey, Lee. *Curious Facts*. New York: Holt, Rinehart and Winston, 1980.

Parks, Lillian Rogers, in collaboration with Leighton, Frances Spatz. *The Roosevelts: A Family in Turmoil*. Englewood Cliffs, N.J.: Prentice-Hall, 1981.

Shenkman, Richard, and Reiger, Kurt. *One-Night Stands with American History: Odd, Amusing, and Little-Known Incidents*. New York: William Morrow & Co., 1980.

Storer, Doug. *Encyclopedia of Amazing but True Facts*. New York: New American Library, 1980.

Tugwell, Rexford G. *How They Became President; Thirty-five Ways to the White House*. New York: Simon and Schuster, 1964.

Webster's Guide to American History. Springfield, Mass.: G. & C. Merriam Co., 1971.

Whitney, David C. *The American Presidents*, Garden City, N.Y.: Doubleday & Co., 1982.

Mothers

Butterfield, L.H., Friedlaender, Marc, and Kline, Mary-Jo, Eds. *The Book of Abigail and John: Selected Letters of the Adams Family 1762-1784*. Cambridge, Harvard University Press, 1975.

SOURCES

Cunliffe, Marcus. *George Washington: Man and Monuments.* New York: New American Library, Mentor Books, 1958.
Faber, Doris. *The Presidents' Mothers.* New York: St. Martin's Press, 1976.
Lorant, Stefan. *The Life and Times of Theodore Roosevelt.* Garden City, N.Y., Doubleday & Co., 1959.
Reedy, George. *Lyndon B. Johnson: A Memoir.* New York and Kansas City: Andrews and McMeel, 1982.
Wilson, Dorothy Clarke. *Lincoln's Mothers.* Garden City. N.Y.: Doubleday & Co., 1981.

Fathers

Beschloss, Michael R. *Kennedy and Roosevelt: The Uneasy Alliance.* New York: W. W. Norton & Co., 1980.
Brayman, Harold. *From Grover Cleveland to Gerald Ford . . . The President Speaks Off-The-Record.* Princeton, N.J.: Dow Jones Books, 1976.
The Letters of Archie Butt: Personal Aide to President Roosevelt. Edited by Abbott, Lawrence F. Garden City, N.Y.: Doubleday, Page & Co., 1924.
Parmet, Herbert S. *Jack: The Struggles of John F. Kennedy.* New York: Dial Press, 1980.
Reagan, Ronald. *Where's the Rest of Me?* with Hubler, Richard G. New York: Karz Publishers, 1981.
Roosevelt, Theodore. *An Autobiography.* New York, Charles Scribner's Sons, 1926.
Russell, Francis. *The Shadow of Blooming Grove: Warren G. Harding in His Times.* New York, McGraw-Hill, 1968.
Valenti, Jack. *A Very Human President,* New York: W. W. Norton, 1975.

Brothers and Sisters

Abrahamsen, David, M.D. *Nixon vs. Nixon: An Emotional Tragedy.* New York: Farrar, Straus and Giroux, 1976.
Forer, Lucille K., Ph.D. with Still, Henry. *The Birth Order Factor: How Your Personality is Influenced by Your Place in the Family.* New York: Pocket Books, 1977.
Jencks, Christopher; Bartlett, Susan; Corcoran, Mary; Crouse, James; Eaglesfield, David; Jackson, Gregory; McClelland, Kent; Mueser, Peter; Olneck, Michael; Schwartz, Joseph; Ward, Sherry, and Williams, Jill. *Who Gets Ahead? The*

181

Determinants of Economic Success in America. New York: Basic Books, 1979.

Konitzer, Bela. *The Real Nixon: An Intimate Biography.* Chicago: Rand McNally, 1960.

Stapleton, Ruth Carter. *Brother Billy.* New York: Harper & Row, 1978.

Tarshis, Barry. *The "Average American" Book.* New York: Atheneum/SMI, 1979.

Names

Burke's Presidential Families of the United States of America, First Edition London; Burke's Peerage, 1975.

Ford, Gerald R. *A Time to Heal.* New York: Harper & Row and Reader's Digest, 1979.

Reeves, Richard. *A Ford, not a Lincoln.* New York: Harcourt Brace Jovanovich, 1975.

The United States Presidents: Their Lives, Families and Great Decisions. Edited by the Saturday Evening Post. Indianapolis, Ind.: Curtis Publishing, 1980.

Prophecies

If Elected. . . Presidential Campaigns from Lincoln to Ford as Reported by the New York Times. Edited by Keylin, Arleen, and Nelson, Eve. New York: Arno Press, Random House, 1976.

Oates, Stephen B. *With Malice Toward None: The Life of Abraham Lincoln.* New York, Harper & Row, 1977.

Sandburg, Carl. *Abraham Lincoln: The Prairie Years, Vols. I & II.* New York, Harcourt, Brace & World. 1926.

Wayne, Stephen J. *The Road to the White House: The Politics of Presidential Elections.* New York: St. Martin's Press, 1980.

Education

Carter, Jimmy. *Why Not the Best?* Nashville, Tennessee: Broadman Press, 1975.

SOURCES

Greenstein, Fred I. *The Hidden-Hand Presidency: Eisenhower as Leader.* New York: Basic Books, 1982.
Ketchum, Richard M. *The World of George Washington.* New York, American Heritage Publishing, 1974.
Koch, Adrienne, and Peden, William, Eds. *The Life and Selected Writings of Thomas Jefferson.* New York, Modern Library, 1944.
Morris, Edmund. *The Rise of Theodore Roosevelt.* New York, Coward, McCann & Geoghegan, 1979.
Norton, Howard, and Slosser, Bob. *The Miracle of Jimmy Carter.* Plainfield, N.J.: Logos International, 1976.

Businesses

David, Burke. *Old Hickory: A Life of Andrew Jackson.* New York, Dial Press, 1977.
Donovan, Robert J. *Conflict and Crisis: The Presidency of Harry S Truman, 1945–1948.* New York: W. W. Norton & Co., 1977.
Flexner, James Thomas. "George Washington, Businessman." *American Heritage* XVI, no. 6 (October 1965): 94–98.
Grant, Ulysses S. *Personal Memoirs, Vol I.* New York, Charles L. Webster & Co., 1885.
Miller, Merle. *Plain Speaking: An Oral Biography of Harry S. Truman.* New York: Berkley Publishing, 1973.
Remini, Robert V. *Andrew Jackson and the Course of American Empire, 1767–1821.* New York, Harper & Row, 1977.
Slappey, Sterling G. "100th FDR Anniversary to Focus on Hyde Park," *Chicago Tribune,* 17 January 1982, Sec. 11:9–10.

Pets

Bryant, Traphes, with Leighton, Frances Spatz. *Dog Days at the White House.* New York, Macmillan, 1975.
Kunhardt, Dorothy Meserve, and Kunhardt, Philip B., Jr. *Twenty Days: A Narrative in Text and Pictures of the Assassination of Abraham Lincoln and the Twenty Days and Nights that Followed—The Nation in Mourning, the Long Trip Home to Springfield.* Secaucus, N.J., Castle Books, 1965.

Truman, Margaret. *White House Pets.* New York: David McKay Co., 1969.

Wives

Barton, William E. *The Women Lincoln Loved.* Indianapolis, Bobbs-Merrill Co., 1927.

David, Lester, and David, Irene. *Ike and Mamie: The Story of the General and His Lady.* New York: G.P. Putman's Sons, 1981.

Klaphtor, Margaret Brown. *The First Ladies.* Washington, D.C.: White House Historical Assoc. and National Geographic Society, 1975.

Leamer, Laurence. *Make-Believe; The Story of Nancy & Ronald Reagan.* New York: Harper & Row, 1983.

McConnell, Jane and Burt. *Our First Ladies: From Martha Washington to Pat Ryan Nixon.* New York: Thomas Y. Crowell, 1969.

Morris, Sylvia Jukes. *Edith Kermit Roosevelt: Portrait of a First Lady.* New York: Coward, McCann & Geoghegan, 1980.

Robbins, Jhan. *Bess & Harry; An American Love Story.* New York: G. P. Putnam's Sons, 1980.

Simon, John Y., ed. *The Personal Memoirs of Julia Dent Grant (Mrs. Ulysses S. Grant).* New York: G. P. Putnam's Sons, 1975.

Withey, Lynne. *Dearest Friend: A Life of Abigail Adams.* New York: Fress Press, 1981.

West, J.B., with Kotz, Mary Lynn. *Upstairs at the White House: My Life with the First Ladies.* New York: Coward, McCann & Geoghegan, 1973.

Children

Ayres, B. Drummond, Jr. "Thomas Jefferson's Descendants Continue to Serve," *New York Times,* 5 July 1976.

Bishop, Joseph Bucklin, Ed. *Theodore Roosevelt's Letters to His Children.* New York, Charles Scribner's Sons, 1919.

Brough, James. *Princess Alice: A Biography of Alice Roosevelt Longworth.* Boston: Little, Brown and Co., 1975.

Brown, Gene, ed. *The Kennedys: A New York Times Profile.* New York: Arno Press, 1980.

Canfield, Cass. *The Iron Will of Jefferson Davis.* New York: Fairfax Press, 1978.

Eisenhower, John S.D. *Strictly Personal,* Garden City, N.Y.: Doubleday & Co., 1974.

Eisenhower, Julie Nixon, "Teddy Roosevelt's Daughter at 90." *Saturday Evening Post,* March 74:42.

Palmer, Alan. *Kings and Queens of England.* London: Octopus, 1976.

Truman, Margaret. *Letters from Father: The Truman Family's Personal Correspondence.* New York: Arbor House, 1981.

Vidal, Gore; Pritchett, V.S.; Caute, David; Chatwin, Bruce; Conrad, Peter; Epstein, Edward Jay. *Great American Families.* New York: W. W. Norton & Co., 1977.

Wallace, Robert. "If Washington Had Become King." *Life,* 19 February 1951:107–114.

Health

Bollet, Alfred Jay, M.D. "Franklin D. Roosevelt and Poliomyelitis." *Resident & Staff Physician,* December 1983: 93–104.

Bollet, Alfred Jay, M.D. "Wounded Presidents: 1981 Almost Repeats the Events of 1881." *Residents & Staff Physician,* May 1981: 33–36.

Marmor, Michael F., M.D. *"Wilson, Strokes, and Zebras." New England Journal of Medicine* Vol. 307, No. 9 (26 August 1982):528–535.

Mistresses and Girlfriends

Adler, Bill, with King, Norman. *All in the First Family: The Presidents' Kinfolk.* New York: G. P. Putnam's Sons, 1982.

Bailey, Thomas A. *Presidential Saints and Sinners.* New York: Macmillan, 1981.

Benjamin Franklin's Autobiography, Edited by W. Macdonald. New York: Everyman's Library, 1968.

Bradlee, Benjamin C. *Conversations with Kennedy.* New York: W.W Norton & Co., 1975.

Dabney, Virginius. *The Jefferson Scandals: A Rebuttal.* New York, Dodd, Mead & Co., 1981.

McAdoo, Eleanor Wilson. "The Courtship of Woodrow Wilson." *American Heritage* XIII, no. 6 (October 1962):28.

Miller, Hope Ridings. *Scandals in the Highest Office: Facts and Fictions in the Private Lives of Our Presidents.* New York: Random House, 1973.

Morgan, Kay Summersby. *Past Forgetting: My Love Affair with*

Dwight D. Eisenhower. New York: Simon and Schuster, 1975.
Saunders, Frank, with Southwood, James. *Torn Lace Curtain.* New York: Holt, Rinehart and Winston, 1982
Schachtman, Tom. *Edith & Woodrow: A Presidential Romance.* New York, G.P. Putnam's Sons, 1981.
Tansill, Charles Callan. *The Secret Loves of the Founding Fathers: The Romantic Side of George Washington, Thomas Jefferson, Benjamin Franklin, Gouverneur Morris, Alexander Hamilton.* New York: Devin-Adair Co., 1964.
Tribble, Edwin, Ed. *A President in Love: The Courtship Letters of Woodrow Wilson and Edith Bolling Galt.* Boston, Houghton Mifflin, 1981.

Foods

Hazelton, Jean Janvey. "Thomas Jefferson, Gourmet." *American Heritage* XV, no. 6 (October, 1964):20.
Kimball, Marie. *Thomas Jefferson's Cook Book.* Charlottesville: University Press of Virginia, 1976.
Klaphtor, Margaret Brown. *The First Ladies Cook Book: Favorite Recipes of All the Presidents of the United States.* Edited by Bullock, Helen Duprey. New York: Parents Magazine Enterprises, 1982.
Lippman, Theo, Jr. *The Squire of Warm Springs: F.D.R. in Georgia 1924–1945.* Chicago: Playboy Press, 1977.
Lossing, Benson J. *George Washington's Mount Vernone or Mount Vernon and Its Associations, Historical, Biographical, and Pictorial.* New York: Fairfax Press, n.d.
Reuben, David, M.D. *Everything You Always Wanted to Know About Nutrition.* New York: Avon, 1978.
Rodale, J.I., and Staff. *The Complete Book of Vitamins.* Emmaus, Penn.: Rodale Books, 1976.
Root, Waverley, and de Rochemont, Richard. *Eating in America: A History.* New York: William Morrow and Co., 1976.
Tannahill, Reay. *Food in History.* New York: Stein and Day, 1973.

Ancestors and Relatives

Burke's Presidential Families of the United States of America, First Edition. London: Burke's Peerage, 1975.

SOURCES

Hart, Michael H. *The 100: A Ranking of the Most Influential Persons in History.* New York: A & W Visual Library, 1978.
Jensen, Oliver. " 'We are All Descended from Grandfathers!' " *American Heritage* XV, no. 4(June 1964):4–13.
McGinnis, Ralph Y., Ed. *Quotations from Abraham Lincoln.* Chicago, Nelson-Hall, 1977.
Miller, Nathan. *The Roosevelt Chronicles.* New York, Doubleday & Company, Inc., 1979
Morris, Dan and Inez. *Who Was Who in American Politics.* New York: Hawthorn Books, 1974.
Nagel, Paul C. *Descent from Glory: Four Generations of the John Adams Family.* New York, Oxford University Press, 1983.
Ross, Ishbel. *An American Family: The Tafts—1678 to 1964.* Cleveland and New York: World Publishing, 1964.
Russell, Francis. "Honey Fitz." *American Heritage* XIX, no. 5(August 1968):28.
Shepherd, Jack. *The Adams Chronicles: Four Generations of Greatness.* Boston, Little Brown and Co., 1975.

Honesty and Character

Barber, James David. *The Presidential Character: Predicting Performance in the White House,* Second Ed. Englewood Cliffs, N.J.: Prentice-Hall, 1977.
Brodie, Fawn M. *Richard Nixon: The Shaping of His Character.* New York: W. W. Norton & Co., 1981.
Chicago Tribune, 14 January 1982, Sec. 1, p. 7 (F.D.R.'s Taped Conversations)
Dean, John W., III. *Blind Ambition: The White House Years.* New York: Simon and Schuster, 1976.
Findley, Paul. *A. Lincoln: The Crucible of Congress.* New York: Crown Publishers, 1979.
Hayden, Jay G. "Was T.R. a Drunk?" *American Heritage* WV, no. 6(October, 1964):82–90.
Jaros, Dean, and Grant, Lawrence V. *Political Behavior: Choices and Perspectives.* New York: St. Martin's Press, 1974.
Smith, Gene. *High Crimes and Misdemeanors: The Impeachment and Trial of Andrew Johnson.* New York, William Morrow and Co., 1977.
Von Hoffman, Nicholas. *Make-Believe Presidents: Illusions of Power from McKinley to Carter.* New York: Pantheon Books, 1978.

187